KU-346-313

THE
MERRY MUSES
OF
CALEDONIA

MERRY
MUSES
OF
CALEDONIA;

A COLLECTION OF

FAVOURITE SCOTS SONGS,

𝕬𝖓𝖈𝖎𝖊𝖓𝖙 𝖆𝖓𝖉 𝕸𝖔𝖉𝖊𝖗𝖓;

SELECTED FOR USE OF THE
CROCHALLAN FENCIBLES.

Say, Puritan, can it be wrong,
To dress plain truth in witty song?
What honest Nature says, we should do
What every lady does,---or would do.

TITLE PAGE OF ORIGINAL *c.* 1800 EDITION
(Actual size)

Robert Burns

THE MERRY MUSES OF CALEDONIA

Edited by

JAMES BARKE

and

SYDNEY GOODSIR SMITH

*With a Prefatory Note and some authentic
Burns Texts contributed by*

J. DeLANCEY FERGUSON

MACDONALD PUBLISHERS
EDINBURGH

© 1982
Foreword, Prefaces, Text as edited
and Commentaries: the Estates of James Barke,
J. DeLancey Ferguson and Sydney Goodsir Smith;
and M. Macdonald.

ISBN 0 904265 71 4

Published by
Macdonald Publishers
Edgefield Road, Loanhead, Midlothian EH20 9SY

Publication subsidised by
The Scottish Arts Council

374892

Moray District Council
Department of Libraries

821 BUR

Printed in Great Britain by
Macdonald Printers (Edinburgh) Limited
Edgefield Road, Loanhead, Midlothian EH20 9SY

FOREWORD

It is a matter of deepest regret to Professor Ferguson and myself that James Barke, who had been ailing for some time, did not live to see the completion of this book to which he had devoted so much time, research and "honest Scotch enthusiasm." He died aged fifty-two in March, 1958, mourned by lovers of Burns the world over. His Introduction was left in the form of a rough draft, which I have only touched here and there in the way of punctuation and arrangement.

It was a chance remark of my friend and fellow Burnsian, Mr. Maurice Lindsay, that led me to Lord Rosebery's unique copy of the original *c.* 1800 edition of *The Merry Muses* that forms the basis of the present edition. To Lord Rosebery's great kindness in giving me access to this precious opusculum I have referred in the course of my Introduction; to Mr. Lindsay also I would tender the gratitude of the editors.

Before this happy chance occurred we had laboured long with the baffling mystery of sometimes as many as six different versions of a particular song—all declaredly taken from the *c.* 1800 edition, from this particular and unique copy of Lord Rosebery's that had belonged to William Scott Douglas. It was Miss Roger of the Dunfermline Public Library who unlocked for me the doors of the innermost secret chambers of the Murison Burns Collection and first displayed to my astonishment the Ewing transcript of this edition that proved to differ so alarmingly from Duncan M'Naught's Burns Federation edition of 1911 and that started off the investigations the fruits of which lie before you now.

Another bouquet must go to Mr. W. N. H. Harding of Chicago, whose collection of old songbooks must be one of the finest in the world and who kindly transcribed for me many songs from his—also unique—copy of *The Giblet Pye* (*c.* 1806). Until we came upon the 1800 edition of the *Muses* these were some of the oldest texts we had.

For other courtesies I must thank Mr. D. M. Lloyd of the National Library of Scotland, Mr. M. C. Pottinger of the Scottish Central Library and Mr. Basil Megaw of the School of Scottish Studies, Edinburgh University.

[5]

Since the first edition of this collection appeared in 1959, my friend and fellow sleuth, Mr. G. Legman, has discovered in the British Museum Library a manuscript by Alan Cunningham which suggests that six songs previously grouped in Section III are actually Burns originals and, in particular, shows that the purified versions of these in the Aldine edition of 1839 are in fact forged expurgations by Cunningham himself. Accordingly, in this new edition, we have transferred these to Section IV. A full discussion of Mr. Legman's important find is not possible here. Scholars are directed to his two extremely interesting essays on the Cunningham MS and *"The Merry Muses* as Folklore" in his *The Horn Book* (University Books Inc., New York, 1964). Which also prints some half dozen hitherto unknown songs and verses by Burns.

Edinburgh, August 1964   S.G.S.

NOTE

Punctuation and style in Sections I and VI follow Burns's holograph. Elsewhere, punctuation as a rule follows the text, but where this was very erratic it has sometimes been emended. Inconsistencies in spelling are literal.

CONTENTS

❦

[9]

ILLUSTRATIONS

SOURCES AND TEXTS
OF THE SUPPRESSED POEMS

❧

By J. DeLancey Ferguson

That Burns collected bawdy folksongs, and added to them,
is a fact not questioned even by the bardolators who strive
to ignore it. He devoted a special notebook to the collection;
his most detailed, and most often quoted, allusion to it occurs
in a letter to John M'Murdo of Drumlanrig which was probably
written in February, 1792:

> I think I once mentioned something to you of a Collection of
> Scots Songs I have for some years been making: I send you a
> perusal of what I have gathered.—I could not conveniently
> spare them above five or six days, and five or six glances of them
> will probably more than suffice you.—When you are tired of
> them please leave them with Mr. Clint of the King's Arms.—
> There is not another copy of the Collection in the world, & I
> should be sorry that any unfortunate negligence should deprive
> me of what has cost me a good deal of pains.—

More than two years earlier, on sending a copy of "I'll Tell
You a Tale of a Wife" to Provost Maxwell of Lochmaben,
the poet had added, "You see, Sir, I have fulfilled my promise:
I wish you would think of fulfilling yours, and come &
see the rest of my Collection.—" He had tried his hand at
original composition of such verses at least as early as 1784,
when he copied "My Girl She's Airy" into his Commonplace
Book: he had begun recording folk bawdry at least as early
as 1786—in other words before he had met James Johnson
and become actively concerned with the *Scots Musical
Museum*. His transcript of "Brose an' Butter" was taken
down on the reverse of a draft letter to Margaret Kennedy of
Daljarrock. That letter was probably written in late autumn,

[15]

1785; the song, on the clear evidence of his handwriting, must have been copied down within the next twelve months or so.

As to what happened to the collection after Burns's death, the earliest version is Robert Chambers's:

> Unluckily, Burns's collection of these facetiae (including his own essays in the same walk) fell . . . into the hands of one of those publishers who would sacrifice the highest interests of humanity to put an additional penny into their own purses; and, to the lasting grief of all the friends of our Poet, they were allowed the honours of the press. The mean-looking volume which resulted should be a warning to all honourable men of letters against the slightest connection with clandestine literature, much more the degradation of contributing to it. . . .

Duncan M'Naught, quoting this passage in his preface to the Burns Federation reprint of *The Merry Muses*, added in a footnote that the collection "was obtained on loan from Mrs. Burns on false pretences, and never returned." He did not document this statement, any more than he documented "the authority of Professor Wilson" for an assertion that Burns, on his deathbed, was offered fifty pounds for the collection and repelled the offer with horror. However, it is always hard to document what never happened, and the real history of Burns's papers was a matter of record long before Robert Chambers's day.

Late in 1796 Dr. James Currie agreed to write a life of Burns, and to edit his works, for the benefit of the poet's widow and children. John Syme, one of Burns's closest friends in Dumfries, undertook to collect documents—all the letters he could induce their recipients to release (that to John M'Murdo, just quoted, was one of them), together with everything handwritten he could find in the poet's home. What he had accumulated he forwarded to Currie in February, 1797. "I received," the Doctor recalled, "the complete sweepings of his drawers and of his desk—as it appeared to me—even to the copy-book on which his little boy had been practising his writing."

Those complete sweepings included whatever notebooks and journals Burns had kept, as well as his loose papers. The

Glenriddell MSS, both the Commonplace Books, the journals of the Border and Highland tours, the notebook which began as farming memoranda and ended as a poetical miscellany— all these are known to have been in Currie's custody. There is no reason to doubt that *The Merry Muses* (call it that for convenience, though there is no proof that the title is Burns's) was included in the consignment. One bit of evidence, indeed, is almost proof-positive that Currie had the collection.

When he printed the much-quoted letter to John M'Murdo, Currie interpolated a sentence which Burns had failed to write: "A very few of them are my own"—a sentence italicized by every apologist from Currie's day to ours. Unless he had seen Burns's manuscript, the editor would have no motive for the forgery. In the letter Burns does not claim *any* of the collection as his own.

These facts cannot be controverted, but they can be ignored. They have been, by all the apologists who cling to the tale that the verses reached print through some scoundrel who fraudulently obtained the manuscript from Jean Burns. These same apologists allege that *The Merry Muses* was printed in, or near, Dumfries about 1800. The paper is water-marked "1800," which provides a *terminus a quo*; if there is any evidence that Dumfries was the place it has not been divulged. But in 1800 the manuscript, unless he had already destroyed it, was still in Currie's hands, in Liverpool, and it is inconceivable that anyone so prudish can have been a party to the publication. He published his edition in that year, but returned none of the papers in his custody. He intended a comprehensive revision and enlargement of his work.

That intent was frustrated by his death in 1805, but still the papers were not returned. Some were given away—the farming memoranda book, and other documents as well, were in William Roscoe's library in the 1820's. Some may have been lost or destroyed. Many remained in the hands of Currie's descendants until 1865, when they were sold at auction. The one certainty is that none of them was ever at Jean Burns's disposal after February, 1797. Hence, if *The*

Merry Muses was really printed at Dumfries about 1800, it was printed from some other source than Burns's holograph collection.

I once believed that most of the documents which Currie's successors have failed to locate were destroyed by the Doctor or his heirs. I no longer think so. Though some doubtless perished through carelessness, the slow reappearance in recent years of "lost" manuscripts absolves the Curries from charges of wholesale or deliberate destruction. Currie *may* have felt *The Merry Muses* scandalous enough to demand purification by fire. On the other hand, he may merely have kept the volume under lock and key, as Burns himself did. M'Naught asserted that "what appear to be stray leaves still find their way occasionally into the manuscript market." As usual, he offered no supporting evidence. Bawdy verses by Burns certainly exist in separate holographs as well as in letters, but none that I have seen bears any clear indication, such as page numbers, of deriving from a manuscript volume. The collection *may* have been broken up or destroyed. Equally well, it may still be hidden in the cache where a Victorian owner concealed it from his family. One guess is as good as another.

But if Currie had the original, what was the source of the "1800" volume? One can only conjecture. Before conjecturing, though, one must make certain postulates about the nature and scope of Burns's collection. First, in the case of folksongs, it would obviously contain texts differing little, if at all, from his jottings from oral recitation and from the copies he transcribed for friends. Next, in the case of his own compositions in the genre, the texts would be final ones, not rough drafts; he would be unlikely to enter the verses in the book until they were in a form which satisfied him. Finally, one would expect the volume to include all, or almost all, his own compositions which he viewed as unfit for general circulation. But the "1800" edition conforms to none of these three standards.

Not many of Burns's jottings survive, but the two or three available for comparison all show numerous divergencies from the *Merry Muses* text. Thus his version of "Brose an'

Butter," set down not later than 1786, consists, like that in the *Muses*, of five stanzas and a chorus. But the last two lines of the chorus are different; the stanza order differs; Burns's text lacks the *Muses*' closing stanza but includes a stanza lacking in the *Muses*.

"Cumnock Psalms" was most certainly in Burns's collection: he copied it out, for George Thomson's edification, in 1794. Presumably he had his book in front of him. Yet his version has a different refrain and three lines widely variant from the *Muses*. We know, moreover, that Burns had songs not in the *Muses* at all. In March, 1795, for instance, he quoted to Patrick Miller Jr. "an old Scotish stanza" beginning "There cam a soger here to stay." Obviously it came from his collection. But it is missing in the "1800" *Muses*, only to appear, garbled, as stanza 2 of "The Reels o' Bogie" in the even less authentic edition of 1827. The first editor missed it entirely; the second got it wrong. *Ergo*, neither printed from Burns's holograph.

What applied to the folksongs applies *a fortiori* to Burns's own compositions. Since he often copied from memory, minor textual differences are to be expected; changes of form, and omissions of whole stanzas, are not, if the printer worked from holographs. Yet the *Muses* version of "The Fornicator" has only four stanzas, whereas the one known manuscript has six. The version of "I'll Tell You a Tale of a Wife" which Burns sent to Provost Maxwell on December 20, 1789, has eleven stanzas. The *Muses* text has only eight, and the three that are missing include the best travesty of Calvinistic logic. We have the poet's own word that the song was part of his collection. A printer working from that collection could hardly manage to overlook three whole stanzas.

Equally convincing is the text of "When Princes and Prelates." Of that song two holographs survive, written more than eighteen months apart. Burns composed the song at Sanquhar on December 12, 1792, and sent it off at once to Robert Cleghorn. In July, 1794, he copied it out for George Thomson. This second manuscript differs in only one half-line from the Cleghorn text. But the *Muses* version includes two additional stanzas—one repetitious, the other incompletely rhymed—and has different line structure throughout. Obviously what Burns had written in 1792 still satisfied him in 1794. When, then, is he likely to have reworked the song in a wholly different form?

This argument might be followed through all the verses which survive in holograph, for few of the manuscripts agree *verbatim* and *literatim* with the *Muses*. But equally significant is the absence from the *Muses* of verses which Burns is known to have written or collected. That volume includes three lyrics from "The Jolly Beggars," but none of them is the closing chorus, "A fig for those by law protected." Yet in September, 1793, Burns told George Thomson, "I have forgot the Cantata you allude to, as I kept no copy, & indeed did not know that it was in existence; however, I remember that none of the songs pleased myself, except the last—something about

'Courts for cowards were erected,
'Churches built to please the priest.' "

Even if we assume that the poet, for some obscure reason, was mystifying Thomson, the dilemma remains. If Burns had a copy, and *The Merry Muses* was really printed from his collection, the whole of the "Beggars" should be there. If he told Thomson the truth, the nameless editor must have obtained his texts elsewhere.

Still stranger is the absence of "Holy Willie's Prayer." It never occurred to Burns that that great soliloquy would one day stand among his collected masterpieces, but he knew it was a masterpiece. So did his friends, who were always pestering him for copies. Though it had been printed in a Stewart and Meikle pamphlet in 1799, it was not openly included in his works until 1810; hence it should have rated top billing in the *Muses*. However, "Holy Willie," like "Grizzel Grimme," is not a song; therefore it might not have been in the same notebook with the lyrics. But "My Girl she's airy," "When Prose-work and Rhymes," and "There Was Twa Wives" are most definitely songs, and the two last were composed in the same years as "Act Sederunt" and "When

[20]

Princes and Prelates." If the one pair were copied into the collection, it is hard to understand why the others were not also.

It has taken far too many words to reach a simple conclusion. If *The Merry Muses* was printed in Dumfries or, more likely, Edinburgh in 1800, it could not have been taken from a holograph in Dr. Currie's home in Liverpool. Even if it was printed elsewhere, at another date, it still could not have been taken from the holograph, for the texts are both inaccurate and incomplete. The obvious—and only—alternative is that the *Muses* was compiled from versions set down from memory, or from hasty transcriptions by hands other than the poet's. Plenty of cronies, in Dumfries and elsewhere, could have brought together the collection on those terms, but it is easier to say who probably did not do it than to say who probably did.

The title page dedicates the verses to the Crochallan Fencibles, which suggests an Edinburgh rather than a Dumfries provenance. Traditionally, Robert Cleghorn was the intermediary in transmitting Burns's cloaciniads to the club. But if Cleghorn had had any part at all in the printing, the *Muses* would—to cite only two examples—have included "There Was Twa Wives" and the Cleghorn text of "When Princes and Prelates." Cleghorn, therefore, is ruled out. Had John Syme or Alexander Cunningham been involved, one would expect some hint of the fact in their extant correspondence. It is easy enough to guess at others who *might* have done it: in Dumfries, for instance, Colonel dePeyster or John M'Murdo; in Edinburgh, Charles Hay (later Lord Newton), or the poet's "facetious little friend," William Dunbar, or even Peter Hill. But without clues guessing is useless.

In sum, then, the "1800" edition ceases to have any unique authority. Whatever the course of its contents, it was not printed from Burns's own manuscript collection of bawdy verse. We may have to accept its versions in default of better; we must never trust them.

Our present edition can make no sweeping claim to accuracy or completeness. For about a score of pieces, however, it offers texts directly based on Burns's own manuscripts. That is more than can be said of any of its predecessors.

Falls Village, Connecticut, 1958

NOTE. The contents of the present volume represent a variety of sources and a diversity of editorial opinion. My share in the work consists of this preface and of the texts on which the headnotes bear my initials.—DLF.

PORNOGRAPHY AND BAWDRY IN LITERATURE AND SOCIETY

◦◈◦

By James Barke

The nature of pornography and obscenity in literature is
complex. Its origin dates back to the origin of literature and
to the essential literature concerning sexual characteristics of
man and woman. The aesthetic and sociological aspects of
bawdry are worth some consideration. What, for instance, is
meant exactly by the words pornography and obscenity in
relation to literature in general and poetry and folksong in
particular? The Oxford Dictionary defines pornography as
"licentious writing (Greek porné, harlot)" and obscenity as
". . . indecent, bawdy," but these definitions are subject to
the law of change. Also, they do not *define*. Is *The Song of
Songs* pornographic? What about Dunbar's "Twa Mairrit
Wemen and the Wedow" or John Cleland's *Fanny Hill*? It all
seems to be very much a matter of fashion, of taste, of opin-
ion. I saw Joyce's *Ulysses* denounced in Britain and America
as outrageous pornography. I have lived to see it openly sold
and displayed in British bookshops, and I have read that
it is regarded as essential or even compulsory reading in
universities in the U.S.A.

All of which is very interesting but not very helpful in
attempting to arrive at an understanding of what constitutes
pornography or obscenity. Aesthetic values change, social
values change; bawdry is subject to the same laws as any
other human activity. There never has and never can be ideal
freedom in writing or speech or action. All activity is subject
to what human society at any given time and place permits,
and, in consequence, many artists, frustrated by the ban on

freedom to deal with sexual experience, have had recourse to secret or semi-secret bawdry. Most forms of society have ruthlessly suppressed bawdry while at the same time tolerating a black market in pornography. Against, for example, the nonsexual nature of the Victorian novel stood the underground trade in pornography—much of it of the crudest nature, much of it nauseatingly vile.

Crudity in organizing, in art forms, sexual awareness and sensitivity, has long been with man. In Britain today it finds its most violent expression on the walls of public conveniences. In village, town or city, wherever a convenience affords a blank wall, there will be found, either in word or drawing, the violence, hatred, disgust, nausea, loathing, joy, ecstasy, longing for and ridicule of—sex. And not only in male conveniences; some female conveniences outdo the male in verbal and pictorial sexual expression. The study of this aspect of sexual awareness has not been adequately undertaken in Britain. But the pattern in Scotland, Wales and England seems fairly uniform.

Alongside what might be called urinal art flourishes the art of the smoke-room, taproom story, the smutty tale or joke, the blue story. The appeal of this form of sexual safety valve is common to all sections of society in Britain. I am assured by authorities in America, France, Germany, Poland and Russia that it is equally common with them. There are social nuances of course. There are men who "draw the line" at telling certain types of story in the presence of their wives, or in the company of other women, but who in the company of men know no limits. This is true of women also. The teller of the most crude bawdy stories I ever had the misfortune to know was a Kirk of Scotland elder whose wife, an avid listener, was equally prominent in Kirk work. I have also heard Roman Catholic priests, Kirk of Scotland clergymen, notable lay preachers (Fundamentalist type), learned savants, venerable artists, and other respectable men indulge in the verbal equivalent of urinal art at its crudest.

The creative artist cannot look on all this with equanimity. Bawdy art is bad art in so far as it debases and corrupts the instinct to procreation. Urinal art is bad art. Until very recently the word fuck carried with it, in literature, all the hypnotic power of a verbal atom bomb. In English literature, Lawrence, Joyce, and Henry Miller (to mention a few) have eliminated the hysteria and shock from it. Conversationally, of course, it has always been with us.

"Fuck" I take to be an onomatopoeic word equivalent of the sound made by the penis in the vagina. Here I differ from Mr. Eric Partridge who considers that it denotes violence. It was once an honest enough word and has an honourable history. But early enough in literature it became a taboo word. Today it may be regarded either as the most tender or the most disturbing word in our language.

What applies to fuck is equally relevant to the word cunt—except that it is, poetically, a much harsher word, deriving as it does from the hardening of the Latin *cunus*. But this word, too, had an honest use and has an honourable history. Today, fuck and cunt, and their cognates, are largely used as debased expletives. Their public use, though general in Britain, constitutes an indictable offence—though arrest seldom occurs unless they are bawled out in a public place by a person—not uncommonly a teen-age girl—usually under the influence of alcohol.

But though literary scholars, like medical scholars, must acquire a neutral attitude to the literary and medical aspects of sexual phenomena, the literary scholars must not in any way minimize the effect of words on the untrained ear. The evocative power of a word spoken or printed, like a pictorial image or photograph, can be devastating. I have witnessed a full-grown and responsible adult male become almost insane and undergo profound physical disturbance at being called a bastard. Once in a Highland lochside hotel bar I witnessed a scene that almost amounted to verbal rape. A young red-haired Highland girl was barmaid. A number of middle-class customers were in the bar. Presently a drunken lout entered and demanded a drink. Apparently he had been refused just previously. He looked, in drink, an evil and debauched character. The barmaid politely and firmly refused him a drink. With a viciousness that cannot be conveyed in print he said: "Then gie me a hair frae your dirty big red cunt!"

The effect on the girl was pitiful. Her facial blood vessels seemed as if they would burst on the instant. She clutched the bar and trembled; the expression in her eyes was agonizing. The lout swayed for a moment and then lurched out of the bar as the barmaid, covering her face and sobbing hysterically, ran out from behind the bar into the hotel corridor. I knew the hotel manageress and she told me afterwards that the girl was quite ill for several days.

Certainly the State, the executive power in human society, must exercise the power of censorship to a certain extent, and the more enlightened the State, the more enlightened the censorship. Intellectuals may protest about all forms of control—as I hope they always will—but the fact remains that artistic freedom can never be absolute but must always remain relative and, consequently, ever-changing. We of this generation know only too painfully what bloodlust could be brought to boiling point, torture and bestial mania by the mere incantations of such slogans as Heil Hitler! Perish Judea! and Fuck the Pope! Even the word peace, as Giles the English cartoonist once brilliantly depicted, can in certain circumstances become a dirty and unclean word.

The foregoing observations are necessary before an evaluation of, or even an approach to, Burns's bawdry can be made. This bawdry, of which Burns was legitimately proud, can now be brought into the full light of day. Burns would have welcomed this edition, and I am proud to be associated with it since it establishes to a satisfactory degree just what constitutes Burns's contribution to Scottish bawdry. Scottish bawdry has many peculiar characteristics. It is extremely frank—and it is fundamentally humorous and hence humanistic. It is extremely vigorous and, if it can be said to smell, it smells on the whole like the not unpleasant smell of horse droppings. It reeks of the stable rather than the urinal. To certain olfactory organs it gives the effect of new-mown hay.

To my generation of Scots, Burns, popularly, was the author of two pieces of bawdy doggerel—of which, poetically, he was incapable. On innumerable occasions in the Scottish variety theatre, and sometimes in pantomime, it only required the comedian to give such lines as "The cuddy rins aboot the braes" or "As I stood on the pier o' Leith" to convulse the major part of the audience—especially the married women. One comedian assured me that he had used the "Cuddy" line for thirty years all over Scotland and it had never once failed to bring the house down. Thus, and in other ways, suppression of what Burns actually wrote has resulted in the damnedest obscene trash being ascribed to his pen.

I was brought up in West Fife until I was thirteen years old, in a pleasant household alien to bawdry—or at least inside the four domestic walls. But outside the house, in school and with friends of my own age and upwards to senility, bawdry was general and commonplace: no one gave it much conscious thought. In the school playground, long before puberty, the boys, and sometimes the girls, chanted such bawdy songs as "Mary Ann" (to the tune of "The Girl I Left Behind Me").

> O Mary Ann had a leg like a man
> And a great big hole in her stockin';
> A chest like a drum
> And a big fat bum
> And a hole to shove your cock in!

To the tune of "Cock o' the North" we chanted:

> My Aunt Mary had a canary
> Up the leg o' her drawers,
> For oors and oors
> It cursed the Boers
> And won the Victoria Cross.

And to the tune of "Two Lovely Black Eyes":

> Oor Mary's white drawers,
> Oor Mary's white drawers,
> A hole in the middle
> To let Mary piddle,
> Oor Mary's white drawers.

To "Pop Goes the Weasel":

> Long and thin goes too far in
> And doesn't please the ladies;
> Short and thick does the trick
> And brings out proper babies.

There were many similar bairns' bawdy rhymes, songs and chants common to West Fife in the first two decades of the twentieth century. Comparing notes with a pious Episcopalian approaching his eighties, I found that the identical bairns' bawdry was common to the city of Perth in the 1880s. I must add, however, that the word fuck was so little used as to be almost unknown among school children; and adults rarely or ever used it in the presence of children. Cunt, strangely enough, was commonplace in its legitimate and cognitive use. Sexual intercourse and mutual masturbation were by no means uncommon in the 10–14 age groups. Certain girls were almost nymphomaniacally aggressive. Sexual exhibitionism in classrooms from boys to girls from the age of eight was not uncommon.

The point I wish to stress here is that in Edwardian Scotland there was a universal and firmly established bawdy folk culture in existence, coupled with much seemingly precocious and promiscuous sexual experience. Visual experience of the sexual mating of all animals was debarred to no one of whatever age or sex, except the mating of stallion and mare, which was taboo to all women and children (other than surreptitiously). If, as I have been assured on unimpeachable testimony, the effect on certain otherwise staid and respectable women (married and spinsters) of witnessing the mating of mare and stallion was to induce an almost instantaneous fainting away (orgasm) and an inability to resist the sexual advances of any male who might be on the spot, regardless of age or social condition, then it must be admitted that licentious literature, or any other licentious art form, constitutes highly inflammable and socially dangerous material.

But, socially, I doubt if this problem can be solved by suppression. Pornography and obscenity exist in many art and pseudo-art forms and have a widespread distribution. It obviously caters for a genuine human need. Where art forms are frankest and least suppressed or inhibited, the less the debased or licentious art forms attract. If our educational system were franker and less inhibited, there would be less need for such manifestations as urinal art.

I come back to urinal art. It is universal—in whatever form: *ergo*, it represents a basic human urge; it organizes, after a fashion, something fundamental in the human make-up. Urinal art in Britain exists in its primary, almost primal, condition and in many slightly sublimated or relatively respectable, hence permitted, forms.

Permitted forms today exist in "the living theatre," ice shows, variety shows, illustrated magazines, strip cartoons, and so forth. The pictorial representation of the female bust is a case in point. Even the most decorous and respectable of family newspapers, magazines and journals give prominence to the most exaggerated forms of female breasts. A television walker-on achieved stardom by merely displaying her abnormally developed bosom. She was not permitted to open her mouth—her bust presumably spoke volumes.

It is noteworthy that Burns's bawdry has little or nothing to say in celebration of this part of the female anatomy. Burns could celebrate a "hairy cunt" but he ignored the female breasts. Today, photographers concentrate on these and on the hips and *mon veneris* in bikini or other abbreviated "bathing" dress; Burns's bawdry mainly concentrates on the male and female pudenda. It is remarkably free from any suggestion of perversity, though there is the exaggeration and caricature common to all bawdry. The male tendency to exaggerate the physical aspect of the penis is everywhere in evidence, and he seems to extend to the female the common male belief in the sexual efficacy of an oversized penis. Women are much wiser than this. But the male has ever had the tendency to boast not only of the size of the penis but also of the number of ejaculations achievable in a single bout of intercourse. All this, of course, is normal and quite innocuous: no one other than extreme youth is deceived.

There seems little doubt but that Burns was "well hung"

and was probably what is called oversexed. But sexologists are rightly becoming doubtful as to what constitutes the term oversexed. Some men are capable of regular and repeated acts of vigorous intercourse into their eighties; strong, robust men in their prime border on seeming impotence—without being impotent. There is not yet suffiicent data available to establish a norm; probably there never will be. Women, too, represent all states from the frigid to the nymphomaniac. On balance, however, there does seem to be enough evidence to show that sexual desire is stronger in the female than in the male. If the sexual urge were limited to the act of procreation things would be very different, but the crux of the matter is that the sexual urge is primary, insatiable, irresistible, all-powerful and ruthlessly selfish. Since the processes of defloration and birth are in themselves both unpleasant and dangerous, nature had to make the sexual urge so powerful as to overcome all obstacles of whatever kind or extent. And since man's sexual activity is not governed by seasonal heat the surplus of sexual energy over and above the procreative need is enormous and ever present; and neither starvation nor overwork can kill it. As an appetite, however, sex must be controlled in some fashion for social reasons.

A civilization demands a degree of cleanliness. The need to keep the body clean is based on hygienic and aesthetic considerations. There is an equal need to keep the mind clean— if only for reasons of mental health—but cleanliness has nothing to do with pruriency—or puritanism. The sexual act may be the consummation of love between the sexes, and where the intention is procreative it may be regarded as fulfilling its highest function. Any activity that tends to degrade this supreme function must be regarded as retrogressive and anti-social and essentially pornographic. But it cannot be denied that in modern man sexual activity is also an end in itself—an appetite demanding satisfaction. Ninetenths of sexual activity is of this order.

Against the all-powerful drive to make sex irresistible stand the sanctions of society that limit and suppress free sexual indulgence. Herein lies the social value and significance of bawdry; it provides a safety valve against intellectual and

I'll claſp my arms about your neck,
  As ſouple as an eel, jo;
I'll cleek my houghs about your a--e,
  As I were gaun to ſpeel jo:
I'll cleek my houghs about your a--e,
  As I were gaun to ſpeel, jo;
And if Jock thief he ſhould ſlip out,
  I'll ding him wi' my heel, jo.

Green be the broom on Ellibraes,
  And yellow be the gowan!
My wame it fiſtles ay like flaes,
  As I come o'er the knowe, man:
There I lay glowran to the moon,
  Your mettle wadna daunton,
For hard your hurdies hotch'd aboon,
  While I below lay panting.

"ELLIBANKS"
(from pp. 36, 37 of the 1800 edition, showing Scott Douglas's
emendations)

ANCHOR CLOSE TODAY
by Rendell Wells

The Crochallan Fencibles met in Dawney Douglas's Tavern in this close. There is no contemporary delineation known to us.

emotional sexual pressure and stress. The Scots peasant in singing his bawdy song freed himself from inhibitory pressures and tended to ease sexual tensions—especially through laughter.

It cannot be denied that a society in which urinal art flourishes is in an unhealthy condition: it may even be said, without exaggeration, to be in a dangerously diseased condition. Urinal art and healthy laughing bawdry are two opposite expressions of the primary sexual urge. English bawdry is ever inclined to "snirtle in its sleeve": the prurient snigger is seldom far away. In the main, Scots bawdry is frank, ribald, robustly Rabelaisian, rich in erotic imagery and extraordinarily fanciful in invention.

The flowering of this Scottish art form reached perfection in "The Ball o' Kirriemuir." This ballad-song developed from a twenty-verse work celebrating an actual event to its present-day form in which there are hundreds of verses and innumerable variants. Some thirty years ago a local historian, in the Kirriemuir district, gave me this story of its origin. Around the 1880s a barn dance (harvest-home or kirn dance) was held in the barn of a neighbouring farm. On this occasion the young fellows gathered rose hips and removed the tiny yellow hirsute seeds. These were scattered on the earthen floor of the barn. The girls danced barefooted. Female drawers were not in general use but, where worn, were of the open crotch or "free trade" pattern. In the stour of the dance the small hip seeds lodged around the pudendal hair and set up a pubic and vaginal itch. In other words they constituted a powerful external aphrodisiac. In addition to this, some wag had added a modicum of Spanish fly to the punch bowl. A final touch was the placing of a divot, or sod of grass, in the well of the hanging kerosene lamp. This shortened the life of the illumination to coincide roughly with the time the internal and external aphrodisiacs became effective.

The upshot was an orgy of major proportions and it was this orgy that was celebrated in the original "Ball o' Kirriemuir." Generations of bothy lads embroidered on the original until it was soon impossible to tell where the original began or ended. Two world wars spread it among the personnel of the services and they added and subtracted and amended until today the thing is without beginning or end—and few there are who know anything of its origin.

The original chorus seems to have been:

> Wi' a fa'll dae it this time
> Fa'll dae it noo?
> The yin that did it last time
> Canna dae it noo.

Typical of the original seems to be the verse:

> They were fuckin' in the barn;
> They were fuckin' in the ricks;
> An' ye couldna hear the music
> For the swishin' o' the pricks.

Possibly a contemporary allusion is evinced in

> The minister's wife was there as weel
> A' buckled to the front;
> Wi' a wreath o' roses roun' her airse
> An' thrissels roun' her cunt.

Her daughter was not so protected by this ingenious belt of chastity:

> The minister's dochter tae was there
> An' she gat roarin' fu';
> Sae they doubled her owre the midden wa'
> An' bulled her like a coo.

But if the harvest had been home it would not have been possible for the farmer to bewail this loss:

> Big Rab the fermer cursed and swore
> An' then he roared and grat;
> For his forty acre corn field
> Was nearly fuckit flat.

It is typical of the Scots that when the Highland Division entered Tripoli after the success of the North African campaign, they paraded before Winston Churchill singing verses from "The Ball o' Kirriemuir" in their lustiest voice. The broadcast recording of this historic event had subsequently to be scrapped. It is reported that, at first, Churchill was slightly puzzled by the song but soon broke into "a broad grin."

This indeed is the great leaven that works through almost all Scottish bawdry. It is never sneering or sly or prurient or sexy or titillating. It is almost always blunt and broad and extremely coarse, but seldom vulgar in the music-hall sense; it is never filthy in the sense of the traditional "feelthy postcards." It is seldom refined and, when it is, it is refined in the sense that "The Yellow Yellow Yorlin' " is refined; it is lusty like a good broad bare female buttock.

Burns's bawdry is always coarse, seldom witty, never salacious and not often of a high level. It is unashamedly masculine. There is some evidence of a scatological or coprophilous interest, as in "There Was Twa Wives" and the ballad of "Grizzel Grimme," and in abnormal sexual physiology, as in "Come Cowe Me, Minnie." I confess that when I first read this song, as a youth, it struck me as particularly pointless and coarse. I considered Mary's pudendal peculiarity as altogether imaginary, but when I came to study the physiology and psychology of sex I discovered that Mary's condition was unusual but in no wise unique. Havelock Ellis quotes at least one case where the female pudendal hair was of such a nature as to preclude any attempt at penetration. Again, regarding peculiarities of the male organ, while members of ten, twelve, fourteen or even eighteen inches are not common, they do exist, if infrequently. So that when "The deevil's dizzen Donald drew," i.e. thirteen inches ("Put butter in my Donald's brose"), we cannot accuse the poet of downright lying. Indeed the more we know about sex in all its aspects the more we find that bawdry—at least Scottish folksong bawdry—is guilty of understatement.

On the basis of much experience and long study, I think that in Britain today (and possibly in America, since Britain generally is dominated by American commercial culture) our sexual *mores* represent a profound degeneration of spiritual values and that this is a product of a basely materialistic and commercial civilization. We are living in an age that is hag-ridden by sex—in a degenerate sense. All commercial art tends to exploit and exacerbate the sexual impulse at its most animal level. Pornography and obscenity in its crudest and vilest forms now fail to bring the most tentative blush to the most innocent teen-ager—especially the female. This, of course, where there is adequate strength of character, need not be considered an evil. But when it leads to the physical, mental and spiritual weakening of the individual, then society and the race is correspondingly weakened.

The overall tasks facing society, if society is to endure, demand a high totality of human competence. Hotted-up sex, alcoholism and the need for distraction at animal level (near-nude shows and Marciano-type boxing and so on) spell social decay and the ultimate ruination of civilized society. Sex must be self-disciplined, as eating and drinking must be self-disciplined. And where self-discipline is not effective then there must be some form of social discipline.

On the other hand, sex must be brought out of the dirty bed sheets and fœtid darkness of outmoded inhibitions and taboos. An attitude and approach to sex at once hygienic and social must be deliberately cultivated. We must recognize that the sexual, basically procreative urge is perhaps the most dominant in our life. We must recognize that it is primarily procreative but that the sexual desire and procreative need became divorced many thousands of years ago, that talk of sublimation of the sex urge into higher forms of activity is largely wishful thinking, that unless the female is to be reduced to a round of successive pregnancies and the male to be a slave to a succession of helpless infants, then sex-in-itself must be given a more suitable social outlook other than the foul anti-social outlet of the brothel and the street prostitute.

Contraceptive techniques have removed the fear of the unwanted child and the female need no longer fear the consequences of sexual indulgence. The separation of sex and procreation without recourse to perversion has become absolute. Society is much the healthier for this. Unwanted, unprovided-for children are the tragedy of the earth. There are too many souls in a restricted and ever-shrinking world condemning their parents and ultimately themselves to a treadmill of industrial-commercial slavery and to an ever-intensifying struggle against starvation. But no amount of sociology of this or that "ism" is going to produce the unsexed individual. The sexual interpretation of history proves that the sex impulse will wreck whatever barriers are erected against it.

Until such time as man achieves a civilization based, among other things, on the integration and maximum gratification of the sex impulse, bawdry will provide an invaluable safety valve. There may come a day (and I am still Utopian enough to believe this may be possible) when men and women will live wisely and cleanly and healthily in mind and body and spirit. In that day there will be no need for bawdry as there was no need for it in the Garden of Eden. Even the most sanguine Utopian at his most optimistic realizes that this much-to-be-wished-for day will be a long time a-coming and that it will have to be resolutely, consciously, even desperately striven for. Not so to strive or believe in the validity of the struggle is to turn the face to the wall of life and die.

The old Scots proverb that "a standing cock has nae conscience" is profoundly true, but if civilization is not to relapse, as it has so often relapsed in the past, it must acquire a conscience. Burns, who knew the terrible strength of a standing cock, did much to supply it with such a conscience. Hence his bawdry is never wholly amoral. There is always some moral in it, implicit or explicit. Hence its strength and its glory and its importance for us today. It was not idly that he wrote to Robert Cleghorn: "If that species of Composition be the Sin against the Haly Ghaist 'I am the most offending soul alive.'" And indeed he was—and for the most valid reasons. Certain it is that without an understanding of Burns's bawdry there can be no full understanding of his contribution to history and particularly to the history of the struggle for a society that will ensure the maximum of human happiness.

It may be objected that bawdry has little or nothing to do with sociology. But I do not think that any human activity can be completely divorced from sociological consideration. In any case, I make no apology for raising the issue. Burns himself continually raised it. His personal and social ethic he summed up very neatly in the lines:

> In wars at home I'll shed my blood—
> Life giving wars o' Venus;
> The deities that I adore
> Are social peace and plenty.
> I'm better pleased to mak' one more
> Than be the death o' twenty.

We are his debtors for so much that he has given to the world, and not least for what he did in freeing sex from any taint of sin or shame or guilt or pruriency. In his day perhaps his bawdy verses were indeed, as he said, "not quite ladies' reading" but since then, intellectually at least, women have advanced and they are now as free of the field of bawdry as the men. Maybe they always were. Only today there is little false modesty and a more frank acceptance of equality in this as in so many other fields of activity.

Glasgow, 1958

MERRY MUSES INTRODUCTORY

ᴏ❖ᴏ

By SYDNEY GOODSIR SMITH

As Professor DeLancey Ferguson says, this edition of *The Merry Muses* "can make no sweeping claim to accuracy or completeness"; this will only be possible when Burns's original notebook is discovered. It is an attempt to gather together what has survived of Burns's activities in the field of bawdy song, as author, editor or collector.

In Section I, Professor Ferguson has provided texts from authentic holograph manuscripts of the Bard; the bulk of the rest of the book is taken from the sole surviving copy known of the original *Muses*, now in the possession of the Rt. Hon. the Earl of Rosebery, K.T., and it is due to his lordship's kindness and generosity that we are able to present at last the authentic text of that much-debated volume. The world of Burns scholarship is in his debt, for until now they have seen only garbled nineteenth and early twentieth century versions of this unique collection of Scottish folksong as it existed in Burns's day.

In 1911 Duncan M'Naught produced his famous (or infamous) Burns Federation edition which he stated to have been reproduced from the very volume that now reposes in Lord Rosebery's library (hereinafter called MMC or the 1800 edition—the paper is watermarked 1799 twice and 1800 eight times). A comparison of the two texts will show how far this statement was correct. Not even the contents are the same and the truly enormous number of textual variations are merely "improvements" made by M'Naught or by William Scott Douglas, editor of Burns's *Works* (6 vols., 1877–1879), who once owned this unique copy and who has defaced the pages with numerous alternative readings which M'Naught in his edition has often preferred to the printed text. In this connection it is important to remember that both M'Naught and Scott Douglas were amateur versifiers. An example of Scott Douglas's carryings-on will be seen in Plate 2 ("Ellibanks"); he has obviously just been playing himself.

In the Murison Burns Collection in Dunfermline Public Library there is a transcript of the 1800 edition made by J. C. Ewing "about the year 1893" (according to his note) for an intended edition by W. E. Henley, a project that never matured. Fifty copies of another transcript were made in 1904 for J. S. Farmer, Editor of *Merrie Songs and Ballads Prior to 1800* (1897)—for sale at ten guineas a throw! Both Ewing's and Farmer's transcripts, of the identical Scott Douglas-Rosebery copy, are inaccurate and vary one from another to a considerable degree; both quote Scott Douglas's holograph emendations as "variants." The next stage is for M'Naught in his edition of 1911 to prefer these or his own "variants" to the printed text and to incorporate them silently. Sometimes they correspond to the corrupt versions in the 1827 edition which it was M'Naught's laudable intention to expose as fraudulent. This present edition is the first to reproduce the 1800 texts *verbatim et literatim.* On the only occasion ("The Fornicator") when we have a Burns holograph of verses printed in MMC 1800 and there amended by Scott Douglas, we find the printed text—of the stanzas common to both—corresponds to Burns's and differs from Douglas's.

Here, I must gently and with respect differ from Professor Ferguson when he says, "In the case of folksongs [Burns's notebook] would obviously contain texts differing little, if at all, from his jottings from oral recitation and from the copies he transcribed for friends. In the case of his own compositions in the genre, the texts would be final ones, not rough drafts; he would be unlikely to enter verses in the book until they were in a form which satisfied him." I am afraid poets are not always like that; some are aye tinkering with "final" versions; Burns's own texts vary between the Kilmarnock and Edinburgh editions. In modern times, W. B. Yeats rewrote many of his early poems when publishing his *Collected Works*, and, more recently, Mr. W. H. Auden has done the same. In the case of folksong Burns might easily improve or alter a line here and there when transcribing them for friends; he was not a twentieth century scholar or even an unimaginative and earnest collector like David Herd; he was a poet. However, this is not an important point.

One day, maybe, Burns's notebook will come to light and we shall know all. In the meantime, we offer you this approximation. The contents of the present edition might be described as an "ideal" *Merry Muses*—what might or conceivably could be found if Burns's notebook were discovered. To make room for sixteen new items we have jettisoned ten songs from the 1800 edition which are available in the ordinary editions, *viz.*, those from "The Jolly Beggars" ("I Am a Bard," "Let Me Ryke Up," "I Once Was a Maid") and "The Rantin' Dog the Daddie O't," "Anna," "My Wife's a Wanton Wee Thing," "Beneath a Green Shade," "Wha Is at My Bower Door?" "My Auntie Jean," and "The Cooper o' Cuddy." The new songs are taken either from Burns's own MSS, as in Section I, or from printed sources such as the 1827 edition of the *Muses*, *The Giblet Pye* (*c.* 1806) and David Herd's collections. They are all connected with Burns; either his own work or ascribed to him (Section II) or songs from which he rewrote polite versions. This latter category (Section III) is an important one and central to the collection.

In 1787 in Edinburgh, Burns met James Johnson, an engraver, who "from an honest Scotch enthusiasm [has] set about collecting all our native Songs and setting them to music" (20. 10. 1787). He invited Burns to help him and the Bard entered into the collaboration with enthusiasm—"I have been absolutely crazed about it." He had become a folksong collector—and a folksong writer. From this point on, for the last ten years of his life, this was his chief occupation. Wherever he went, his tours in the Highlands and Borders, doing his rounds as exciseman in Galloway, he jotted down songs and fragments that he heard, to be worked up later into presentable shape for Johnson's *Scots Musical Museum* (6 vols., 1787–1803), and later George Thomson's *Select Collection of Original Scottish Airs* (5 vols., 1793–1826). Many of these, if not most, would be bawdy and many would find a place in his Notebook.

> With a strange contradiction to the grave and religious character of the Scottish people, they possessed a wonderful quantity of indecorous traditionary verse, not of an inflammatory nature, but simply expressive of a profound sense of the ludicrous in connection with the sexual affections. Such things, usually kept from public view, oozed out in the merry companies such as Burns loved to frequent.

Thus Robert Chambers in his *Life and Works of Robert Burns* (1851–52). One such merry company where the non-inflammatory verse "oozed out" were the Crochallan Fencibles, a drinking club of which Burns was a member, who met at Dawney Douglas's tavern in the Anchor Close off the High Street of Edinburgh. It was for them the *Muses* were ostensibly put together.

In Section III there are nearly thirty such songs which Burns transmuted into polite versions and which in their new form have travelled the world over. In Section IV there are another thirty-odd titles which, had he lived longer, might likewise have found their way into decorous society. The polite must never contemn their indecorous beginnings; all our beginnings are, to Holy Willie, "indecorous." Enough of that. Apart from collecting, Burns occasionally tried his own hand at the game, and what we know of these will be found in Sections I and II. By and large, as Henley has pointed out, they are not much superior to the genuine folk examples—if such a category can be defined, for we are all folk. To this the rider should be added that in copying into his notebook a folksong received from, say, a ploughman, Burns has often, demonstrably, tidied it up a bit. In a few cases we can compare his version with that of a contemporary collector who was not a poet, David Herd (*viz.*, "Jockey Was a Bonnie Lad"). In one or two cases he wrote a bawdy version of his own as well as producing a purified one for the drawing rooms ("Had I the Wyte?").

In Section II we have perhaps been overgenerous in our ascriptions. Where there is real evidence that these are Burns's own work we have said so; in other cases the ascriptions are merely the opinions of different editors such as Henley and Henderson, Hecht, Scott Douglas or ourselves. Scott Douglas may have been an irresponsible editor in some ways, but he had a flair for Burns and on occasions his unsubstantiated notions have subsequently been proved documentarily—as in "Nine Inch Will Please a Lady"—so we decided to cite his attributions when we have agreed with him. I should point out here that when I say "we" I mean James Barke and myself; Professor Ferguson is a scholar such as we are not and is rightly suspicious of all such ascriptions unbacked by documentary evidence. For this reason, his contribution to the present volume is by his own request limited to Section I and "The Libel Summons."

As to the poetic value of these songs, apart from their importance in literary history, folklore and sociology—or even maybe anthropology and psychology—opinions must differ. Their biographical value is indubitable; we cannot know Burns completely without them. The Burns, who wrote that masterpiece of sentiment "John Anderson, My Jo, John" was the same Burns who collected and transcribed the "John Anderson" in this book; the Burns who wrote "Had I the Wyte?" in the *Collected Poems* is the same Burns who wrote the version in these pages. We are none of us all pure or all impure, but few are honest or indiscreet enough to let our right hand know what our left hand doeth; maybe we are all of us merely, in Tallulah Bankhead's deathless words, "pure as driven slush." Byron, on reading some of these songs in Burns's then unpublished letters, commented in his journal (13. 12. 1813), "What an antithetical mind!—tenderness, roughness—delicacy, coarseness—sentiment, sensuality—soaring and grovelling, dirt and deity—all mixed up in that one compound of inspired clay!" A true observation and one that could well be applied to the Scots genius as a whole.

Certainly, as a writer, Burns is one of the frankest—or most indiscreet, depending on how you look on it—in history. This grandiosity of indiscretion he shares with Byron and Dunbar, in our own literature, and with Villon and Catullus, Belli and (in a sentimental way) Whitman, in others. To these names we might add Donne, Shakespeare and Rabelais—in their

[41]

very different but all very human ways. In this regard I would quote Whitman's reference to the *Merry Muses* (for which I am indebted to another *grand indiscret*, Mr. Hugh MacDiarmid):

> In these compositions . . . there is much indelicacy . . . but the composer reigns alone, with handling free and broad and true, and is an artist . . . Though so much is to be said in the way of fault-finding, drawing black marks, and doubtless severe literary criticism, after full retrospect of his works and life, the aforesaid "odd kind chiel" remains to my heart and brain as almost the tenderest, manliest, and (even if contradictory) dearest flesh-and-blood figure in all the streams and clusters of by-gone poets. (*Nonesuch* edn., ed. E. Holloway, 825–833)

"Dearest flesh-and-blood figure"—that is a right word, I think, and it is probably this quality that has given Burns his peculiarly affectionate fame among the Scots and, for all I know, elsewhere. His undisguised enjoyment of bawdry, which we all share but not always admit, is part of this open humanity that endears him to us. As James Barke says, there is nothing prurient or sniggering in these songs, nothing either, in Chambers's words, "of an inflammatory character" —they are hearty uninhibited belly laughs. It is a mercy they have survived; they are a unique relic of their period, far superior to their somewhat mawkish English, Anglo-Irish and Anglo-Scottish contemporaries ("Una's Lock" in this volume is typical of these); and we should be poorer without them. As Burns wrote to James Hoy in 1787 (enclosing "one or two poetic bagatelles which the world have not seen, or, perhaps, for obvious reasons, cannot see"), "they may make you laugh a little, which, on the whole, is no bad way of spending one's precious hours and still more precious breath." And who could disagree with that?

Edinburgh, 1958

ABBREVIATIONS

Ald	*Poetical Works of Robert Burns* (ed. George A. Aitken), Aldine Edition, Wm. Pickering, London 1839 and 1893.
Archiv	*Archiv fur das Studium der neueren Sprachen und Literaturen,* cxxix, 363–374; cxxx, 57–72.
B.Chr.	*Robert Burns Chronicle,* Burns Federation, Kilmarnock.
DH	David Herd, *The Ancient and Modern Scots Songs, Heroic Ballads &c,* Edinburgh 1769, 1776 and 1791.
DLF	J. DeLancey Ferguson.
DLF.*L*	J. DeLancey Ferguson, *The Letters of Robert Burns,* edited from the original manuscripts, Oxford, 1931.
Giblet	*The Giblet Pye,* / being the / Heads, Tails, Legs and Wings, / of the Anacreontic songs of the celebrated / R. Burns, G. A. Stevens, Rochester, T. L–tle, / and others. / Some of which are taken from the Original Manus/cripts of R. Burns, never before published / . . . Shamborough: / Printed by John Nox / . . . (*c.* 1806).
GL	G. Legman, *The Horn Book,* New York 1964.
HH	W. E. Henley and T. F. Henderson, *The Poetry of Robert Burns,* Edinburgh, 1896 (Centenary Edition).
Ht.Hd.	Hans Hecht, *Songs from David Herd's MSS,* Edinburgh, 1904.
JB	James Barke.
JCD.*N*	J. C. Dick, *Notes of Scottish Song by Robert Burns, written in an Interleaved Copy* of *The Scots Musical Museum,* London, 1908.
JCD.*S*	J. C. Dick, *The Songs of Robert Burns, with the Melodies for which they were written,* London, 1903.
JCE	J. C. Ewing's transcript of *The Merry Muses of Caledonia* "Dumfries *c.* 1800," in the Murison Burns Collection, Dunfermline.
JSF	J. S. Farmer, *Merrie Songs and Ballads Prior to 1800,* Privately Printed, 1897.
MM27	*The Merry Muses,* a Choice Collection of Favourite Songs from many Sources by Robert Burns [predated], 1827.
MMC	*Merry Muses of Caledonia*; A Collection of Favourite Scots Songs, Ancient and Modern; Selected for use of the Crochallan Fencibles. Undated (*c.* 1800).
M'N	*The Merry Muses of Caledonia*; (Original Edition) A Collection of Favourite Scots Songs Ancient and Modern; Selected for use of the Crochallan Fencibles. . . . A Vindication of Robert Burns in connection with the above publication and the spurious editions which succeeded it. Printed and Published under the Auspices of the Burns Federation. For Subscribers

Only. Not for Sale. 1911. "Introductory and Corrective" by
Vindex [Duncan M'Naught].

MP   *Modern Philology*, xxx, 1, August, 1932 (New York, N.Y.).
PMLA   *Publications of the Modern Language Association of America*
       LI 4; December, 1936 (New York, N.Y.).
SD   W. Scott Douglas, annotator of MMC (*q.v.*).
SGS   Sydney Goodsir Smith.
SMM   James Johnson, *The Scots Musical Museum*, Consisting of Six
       Hundred Scots Songs (Edinburgh 1787). New Edition ed.
       Wm. Stenhouse, Edinburgh, 1853.
TTM   *The Tea-Table Miscellany*, Edinburgh: Printed by Mr. Thomas
       Ruddiman for Allan Ramsay . . . 1724. Also Dublin 1729, and
       Tenth Edition, London, 1740.

I

❦

IN BURNS'S
HOLOGRAPH

The Notes in this section are by
Professor DeLancey Ferguson (DLF)
unless otherwise initialled.

A. *By Burns*

I'LL TELL YOU A TALE OF A WIFE

TUNE: *Auld Sir Symon*

◇

MS formerly in collection of Mr. Lucius Wilmerding, New York.
Burns sent this song to Provost Robert Maxwell of Loch-
maben, December 20, 1789, with this prefatory note:

> . . . I shall betake myself to a subject ever fertile of
> themes, a Subject, the turtle-feast of the Sons of Satan, and
> the delicious, secret Sugar-plumb of the Babes of Grace; a
> Subject, sparkling with all the jewels that Wit can find in
> the mines of Genius, and pregnant with all the stores of
> Learning, from Moses & Confucius to Franklin & Priestly—
> in short, may it please your Lordship, I intend to write
> BAUDY!

At the end of the song, he added:

> You see, Sir, I have fulfilled my promise: I wish you would
> think of fulfilling yours, and come & see the rest of my Col-
> lection.—(DLF, *L* I, 337)

Among the accessible extant MSS, this is the only one which
Burns definitely describes as part of his "Collection." It is
therefore highly significant that the text in *The Merry Muses,*
where it is entitled "The Case of Conscience," lacks stanzas 3,
6 and 7—fairly conclusive evidence in itself that the printed
text could not have been taken from the poet's own notebook.
[DLF]

Catherine Carswell considers this "infamous and ludicrous"
song to have been inspired by Clarinda. [SGS]

◇

I'll tell you a tale of a Wife,
  And she was a Whig and a Saunt;
She liv'd a most sanctify'd life,
  But whyles she was fash'd wi' her ——.—
    Fal lal &c.

[47]

2

Poor woman! she gaed to the Priest,
  And till him she made her complaint;
"There's naething that troubles my breast
  "Sae sair as the sins o' my ——.—

3

"Sin that I was herdin at hame,
  "Till now I'm three score & ayont,
"I own it wi' sin & wi' shame
  "I've led a sad life wi' my ——.—

4

He bade her to clear up her brow,
  And no be discourag'd upon 't;
For holy gude women enow
  Were mony times waur't wi' their ——.—

5

It's naught but Beelzebub's art,
  But that's the mair sign of a saunt,
He kens that ye're pure at the heart,
  Sae levels his darts at your ——.—

6

What signifies Morals & Works,
  Our works are no wordy a runt!
It's Faith that is sound, orthodox
  That covers the fauts o' your ——.—

7

Were ye o' the Reprobate race
  Created to sin & be brunt,
O then it would alter the case
  If ye should gae wrang wi' your ——.—

8

But you that is Called & Free
  Elekit & chosen a saunt,
Will't break the Eternal Decree
  Whatever ye do wi' your ——?—

9

And now with a sanctify'd kiss
  Let's kneel & renew covenant:
It's this—and it's this—and it's this—
  That settles the pride o' your ——.—

10

Devotion blew up to a flame;
  No words can do justice upon't;
The honest auld woman gaed hame
  Rejoicing and clawin her ——.—

11

Then high to her memory charge;
  And may he who takes it affront,
Still ride in Love's channel at large,
  And never make port in a ——!!!*

---

* In a letter to Robert Ainslie, July 29, 1787 (PMLA, LI, 4), Burns quotes what appears to be an alternative final stanza:

  Then, hey, for a merry good fellow;
    And hey, for a glass of good strunt;
  May never we SONS OF APOLLO
    E'er want a good friend and a ——.

St. 4, line 3. *MMC*   For haly gude . . .
St. 5, line 1. *Ibid.*   It's nocht . . .
St. 5, line 4. *Ibid.*   Sae he levels . . .
St. 10, line 3. *Ibid.*   . . . auld carlin . . .
St. 11, line 2. *Ibid.*   And may he wha taks it . . .

[SGS]

D
[49][49]

BONIE MARY

TUNE: *Minnie's ay glowering o'er me—*

❖

MS formerly in Bixby Collection, St. Louis. On October 25, 1793 (?), Burns sent this song, and "Act Sederunt of the Session," to Robert Cleghorn "in all the sincerity of a brace of honest Port" (DLF, *L* II, 212). His preface is well known:

> There is, there must be, some truth in original sin.—My violent propensity to B—dy convinces me of it.—Lack a day! if that species of Composition be the Sin against "the Haly Ghaist," "I am the most offending soul alive."—Mair for taiken, A fine chiel, a hand-wail'd friend & crony o' my ain, gat o'er the lugs in loove wi' a braw, bonie, fodgel hizzie frae the English-side, weel-ken'd i' the brugh of Annan by the name o', Bonie Mary, & I tauld the tale as follows.— N.B. The chorus is auld—

Since Burns alleges a personal basis for the song, a conjectural identification of "Wattie" is Walter Auld, saddler in Dumfries, who occasionally took charge of parcels for the poet in his Ellisland days. The *Scots Magazine* for December, 1793, lists Auld as having been declared bankrupt on December 17. Published in MMC. [DLF]

❖

Chorus—

> Come cowe me, minnie, come cowe me;
> Come cowe me, minnie, come cowe me;
> The hair o' my a— is grown into my c—t,
> And they canna win too [*sic*], to m—we me.

1

When Mary cam over the Border,
When Mary cam over the Border;
As eith 'twas approachin the C—t of a hurchin,
Her a— was in sic a disorder.—

2

But wanton Wattie cam west on't,
But wanton Wattie cam west on't,
He did it sae tickle, he left nae as meikle
'S a spider wad bigget a nest on't.—

3

And was nae Wattie a Clinker,
He m—w'd frae the Queen to the tinkler
Then sat down, in grief, like the Macedon chief
For want o' mae warlds to conquer.—

4

And O, what a jewel was Mary!
And O, what a jewel was Mary!
Her face it was fine, & her bosom divine,
And her c—nt it was theekit wi' glory.—

                    Come cowe &c.

Chorus, line 4. MMC   . . . win in for to . . .
St. 3, line 1. *Ibid.*   . . a blinker

                    [SGS]

ACT SEDERUNT OF THE SESSION

TUNE: *O'er the muir among the heather*

◦◈◦

MS formerly in Bixby Collection, St. Louis. This song was sent
to Robert Cleghorn, October 25, 1793, in the same letter* with
"Come Cowe Me, Minnie" (DLF, *L* II, 212). It was printed,
with some transpositions, in MMC. [DLF]

◦◈◦

A Scots Ballad—

In Edinburgh town they've made a law,
  In Edinburgh at the Court o' Session
That standing pr—cks are fauteors a',
  And guilty of a high transgression.—

Chorus

Act Sederunt o' the Session,
Decreet o' the Court o' Session,
That standing pr—cks are fauteors a',
And guilty of a high transgression.

2

And they've provided dungeons deep.
  Ilk lass has ane in her possession;
Untill the wretches wail and weep,
  They there shall lie for their transgression.—

Chorus

Act Sederunt o' the Session,
Decreet o' the Court o' Session,
The rogues in pouring tears shall weep,
By act Sederunt o' the Session.—

*". . . From my late hours last night, & the dripping fogs & damn'd
east-wind of this stupid day, I have left me as little soul as an oyster.—
'Sir John, you are so fretful, you cannot live long.'—'Why, there is it!
Come, sing me a BAUDY-SONG to make me merry!'—" [Song follows]

[52]

WHEN PRINCES AND PRELATES

TUNE: *The Campbells are Coming*

⟡

Burns composed this song at Sanquhar—after, to judge by the handwriting, a convivial evening—and dispatched it immediately to Robert Cleghorn. The MS is now in the Huntington Library, and is dated December 12, 1792. In July, 1794, Burns sent a copy to George Thomson, eliciting from that usually prim and proper editor the comment, "What a pity this is not publishable" (DLF, *L* II, 250). Both versions consist of six stanzas; apart from variations in spelling, their only important differences are that the Cleghorn text has "people" instead of "folk" and is worded differently in the final stanza, here given in a footnote.

The *Merry Muses* has two additional stanzas, inserted between stanzas 3 and 4, and 4 and 5, respectively, of the present text. In the absence of manuscript authority, these may be considered interpolations. Dumouriez had defeated the Austrians at Jemmappes about a month before Burns wrote the Cleghorn version; the Duke of York stanza could not have been composed before 1793. But both could have been completed long before July, 1794, and if Burns had meant them as part of his final version he would have included them in the Thomson copy. [DLF]

⟡

When princes & prelates & het-headed zealots
  All Europe hae set in a lowe,
The poor man lies down, nor envies a crown,
  And comforts himself with a mowe.—

        Chorus—
  And why shouldna poor folk mowe, mowe, mowe,
    And why shouldna poor folk mowe:
  The great folk hae siller, & houses & lands,
    Poor bodies hae naething but mowe.—

2

When Br—nsw—ck's great Prince cam a cruising to
   Fr—nce,
   Republican billies to cowe,
Bauld Br—nsw—ck's great Prince wad hae shawn
   better sense,
   At hame with his Princess to mowe.—
And why should na &c.

3

Out over the Rhine proud Pr—ss—a wad shine,
   To *spend* his best blood he did vow;
But Frederic had better ne'er forded the water,
   But spent as he docht in a mowe.—
And why &c.

4

By sea & by shore! the Emp—r—r swore,
   In Paris he'd kick up a row;
But Paris sae ready just leugh at the laddie
   And bade him gae tak him a mowe.—
And why &c.

5

Auld Kate laid her claws on poor Stanislaus,
   And Poland has bent like a bow:
May the deil in her a— ram a huge pr—ck o' brass!
   And damn her in h—ll with a mowe!

6

But truce with commotions & new-fangled notions,
   A bumper I trust you'll allow:
Here's George our gude king & Charlotte his queen
   And lang may they tak a gude mowe!*

* In the Cleghorn copy, this stanza reads:

But truth with commotions & new-fangled notions,
   A bumper [I'll fill it I vow (deleted)] I trust you'll allow;
Here's George our good king, & lang may he ring,
   And Charlotte & he tak a mow.—
And why should na &c.

Interpolated stanzas in MMC read:

     When the brave Duke of York
     The Rhine first did pass,
Republican armies to cow, cow, cow,
     They bade him gae hame,
     To his P–ss–n dame,
An' gie her a kiss an' m–w, a m–w.
     And why, &c.

     The black-headed eagle,
     As keen as a beagle,
He hunted o'er height an' o'er howe, howe, howe.
     In the braes of Gemap,
     He fell in a trap,
E'en let him come out as he dow, dow, dow.
     An' why, &c.

WHILE PROSE-WORK AND RHYMES

TUNE: *The Campbells Are Coming*

ᐤ✦ᐤ

Hitherto unpublished. From an original holograph, formerly in the possession of Mr. Owen D. Young, and now in the Berg Collection, New York Public Library. Theme and meter are identical with "When Princes and Prelates." [DLF]

ᐤ✦ᐤ

A Ballad
While Prose-work & rhymes
 Are hunted for crimes,
And things are—the devil knows how;
 Aware o' my rhymes,
 In these kittle times,
The subject I chuse is a ——.

Some cry, Constitution!
 Some cry, Revolution!
And Politics kick up a rowe;
 But Prince & Republic,
 Agree on the Subject,
No treason is in a good ——.

Th' Episcopal lawn,
 And Presbyter band,
Hae lang been to ither a cowe;
 But still the proud Prelate,
 And Presbyter zealot
Agree in an orthodox ——.

Poor Justice, 'tis hinted—
 Ill natur'dly squinted,

The Process—but mum—we'll allow—
    Poor Justice has ever
    For C—t had a favor,
While Justice could tak a gude ——.

Now fill to the brim—
    To her, & to him,
Wha willingly do what they dow;
    And ne'er a poor wench
    Want a friend at a pinch,
Whase failing is only a ——.

NINE INCH WILL PLEASE A LADY

To its ain tune—

ᴏ◈ᴏ

Printed in MMC. M'Naught describes it as "anonymous, but evidently old; perhaps brushed up a little." Nevertheless, in its present form it is probably Burns's own work. Three lines of stanza 1 survive in a fragmentary letter from Ellisland, perhaps addressed to Alexander Dalziel (DLF, *L* I, 295), which is now in the National Library of Scotland. The present text is taken from a photostat of a holograph in the Esty Collection, Ardmore, Pennsylvania. [DLF] In MMC the tune is given as "The Quaker's Wife." [SGS]

ᴏ◈ᴏ

1

"Come rede me, dame, come tell me, dame,
    "My dame come tell me truly,
"What length o' graith, when weel ca'd hame,
    "Will sair a woman duly?"
The carlin clew her wanton tail,
    Her wanton tail sae ready—
I learn'd a sang in Annandale,
    Nine inch will please a lady.—

2

But for a koontrie c—nt like mine,
    In sooth, we're nae sae gentle;
We'll tak tway thumb-bread to the nine,
    And that's a sonsy p—ntle:
O Leeze me on * my Charlie lad,
    I'll ne'er forget my Charlie!
.Tway roarin handfu's and a daud,
  ⸱ He nidge't it in fu' rarely.—

---

* *Leeze me on;* untranslatable expression denoting great pleasure in or affection for a person or thing. [SGS]

But weary fa' the laithron doup,
　And may it ne'er be thrivin!
It's no the length that maks me loup,
　But it's the double drivin.—
Come nidge me, Tam, come nudge me, Tam,
　Come nidge me o'er the nyvel!
Come lowse & lug your battering ram,
　And thrash him at my gyvel!

ODE TO SPRING

TUNE: *The tither morn*

❦

MS, Morgan Library, New York. In January, 1795, Burns wrote to George Thomson (DLF, *L* II, 283):

. . . Give me leave to squeeze in a clever anecdote of my *Spring originality:*—

Some years ago, when I was young, & by no means the saint I am now, I was looking over, in company with a belle lettre friend, a Magazine Ode to Spring, when my friend fell foul of the recurrence of the same thoughts, & offered me a bet that it was impossible to produce an Ode to Spring on an original plan.—I accepted it, & pledged myself to bring in the verdant fields.—the budding flowers,—the chrystal streams,—the melody of the groves,—& a love-story into the bargain, & yet be original. Here follows the piece, & wrote for music too!

The Ode was included in MMC; the present text is from Burns's letter to Thomson. [DLF]

❦

When maukin bucks, at early f——s,
   In dewy grass are seen, Sir;
And birds, on boughs, take off their m——s,
   Amang the leaves sae green, Sir;
Latona's son looks liquorish on
   Dame Nature's grand impètus,
Till his p—go rise, then westward flies
   To r—ger Madame Thetis.

Yon wandering rill that marks the hill,
   And glances o'er the brae, Sir,
Glides by a bower where many a flower
   Sheds fragrance on the day, Sir;

[60]

There Damon lay, with Sylvia gay,
    To love they thought no crime, Sir;
The wild-birds sang, the echoes rang,
    While Damon's a—se beat time, Sir.—

First, wi' the thrush, his thrust & push
    Had compass large & long, Sir;
The blackbird next, his tuneful text,
    Was bolder, clear & strong, Sir;
The linnet's lay came then in play,
    And the lark that soar'd aboon, Sir;
Till Damon, fierce, mistim'd his a——,
    And f——'d quite out of tune, Sir.—

O SAW YE MY MAGGIE?

TUNE: *O Saw ye na my Peggy?*

From holograph MS in the Library of Abbotsford, bound in with Sir Walter Scott's copy of Burns's *The Fornicator's Court*, the flyleaf of which is inscribed anonymously (presumably by the printer or publisher): "Thick paper—only 10 copies printed. To Sir Walter Scott, Bart., June 1823." There is no imprint or colophon. Printed in MMC and there described in a pencilled note by Scott Douglas as "Old." Also appeared MM27. Burns's Note on the song "Saw Ye Nae My Peggie" in the Interleaved SMM (JCD.*N* 4) reads: "This charming song is much older, and indeed much superior to Ramsay's verses, 'The Toast' [TTM 1724, 47], as he calls them. There is another set of the words, much older still, and which I take to be the original one, but though it has a very great deal of merit it is not quite ladies' reading." There is another version in Herd (DH 1769, 175). Although Burns claims this as his own (see footnote) he can only mean "in part." [SGS]

1

Saw ye my Maggie?
Saw ye my Maggie?
Saw ye my Maggie?
 Comin oer the lea?

2

What mark has your Maggie,
What mark has your Maggie,
What mark has your Maggie,
 That ane may ken her be?

[Wry-c—d is she,
Wry-c—d is she,
Wry-c—d is she,
   And pishes gain' her thie.]

3

My Maggie has a mark,
Ye'll find it in the dark,
It's in below her sark,
   A little aboon her knee.

4

What wealth has your Maggie,
What wealth has your Maggie,
What wealth has your Maggie,
   In tocher, gear, or fee?

5

My Maggie has a treasure,
A hidden mine o' pleasure,
I'll howk it at my leisure,
   It's alane for me.

6

How loe ye your Maggy,
How loe [ye] your Maggy,
How loe ye your Maggy,
   An loe nane but she?

7

Ein that tell our wishes,
Eager glowing kisses,
Then diviner blisses,
   In holy ecstacy!—

8

How meet you your Maggie,
How meet you your Maggie,
How meet you your Maggie,
    When nane's to hear or see?

9

Heavenly joys before me,
Rapture trembling o'er me,
Maggie I adore thee,
    On my bended knee!!!

[St. 2a]. This stanza occurs in MMC but not in the MS or in MM27; it might well have been added by Burns when copying the song into his note-book, just as, in the MS, stanzas 6 and 7 are obviously afterthoughts, written in the margin in a different ink, with a different pen, and all stanzas numbered subsequently. The song is here printed in the stanza order in MMC; the numbering is as numbered by Burns in the MS at Abbotsford.

The song is followed by this note in Burns's holograph:

"In the name of Venus, Amen!–Know all men by these Presents, that I, the Author of the foregoing Verses make over and convey from me and my heirs whatever the Copy Right and Property of & in the said Verses to & in favor of, Mr Alexr. Findlater, for his behoof & especially that He, in the hour of Concupiscence, & the power of the Flesh, by giving vent in the channel of Poesy & Song, may keep the said Propensities from hurrying him into the actual momentum of the horrid sin of Uncleanness. –The Author." [SGS]

TO ALEXANDER FINDLATER

Here first printed in full, from a transcript of the original holograph in the Rosebery Collection. The two closing stanzas, and the first four lines of stanza 1, were printed in the Chambers-Wallace *Life and Works of Burns* (Edinburgh, 1896), III, 261–62. *Cf.* DLF, *Letters*, II, 13–14. There seems no reason for assuming, as Wallace did, that these verses and the prose note accompanied the same gift of eggs. [DLF]

Ellisland Saturday morning.

Dear Sir,

our Lucky humbly begs
Ye'll prie her caller, new-laid eggs:
L—d grant the Cock may keep his legs,
     Aboon the Chuckies;
And wi' his kittle, forket clegs,
     Claw weel their dockies!

Had Fate that curst me in her ledger,
A Poet poor, & poorer Gager,
Created me that feather'd Sodger,
     A generous Cock,
How I wad craw & strut and r—ger
     My kecklin Flock!

Buskit wi' mony a bien, braw feather,
I wad defied the warst o' weather:
When corn or bear I could na gather
     To gie my burdies;
I'd treated them wi' caller heather,
     And weel-knooz'd hurdies.

Nae cursed CLERICAL EXCISE
On honest Nature's laws & ties;
Free as the vernal breeze that flies
    At early day,
We'd tasted Nature's richest joys,
    But stint or stay.—

But as this subject's something kittle,
Our wisest way's to say but little;
And while my Muse is at her mettle,
    I am, most fervent,
Or may I die upon a whittle!
    Your Friend & Servant—

        ROBt BURNS

THE FORNICATOR

TUNE: *Clout the Cauldron*

⌖

This song commemorates Burns's amour with Betty Paton, for
which he did public penance in the kirk. The present text is
from a transcript, by the late Davidson Cook, of a MS in the
Honresfield collection. The printed version in MMC gives only
the first four stanzas. [DLF]

⌖

A new Song

Ye jovial boys who love the joys,
    The blissful joys of Lovers,
Yet dare avow, with dauntless brow,
    When the bony lass discovers,
I pray draw near, and lend an ear,
    And welcome in a Frater,
For I've lately been on quarantine,
    A proven Fornicator.

Before the Congregation wide,
    I passed the muster fairly,
My handsome Betsy by my side,
    We gat our ditty rarely;
But my downcast eye did chance to spy
    What made my lips to water,
Those limbs so clean where I between
    Commenc'd a Fornicator.

With rueful face and signs of grace
    I pay'd the buttock-hire,
But the night was dark and thro' the park
    I could not but convoy her;

A parting kiss, I could not less,
  My vows began to scatter,
My Betsy fell—lal de dal lal lal,
  I am a Fornicator.

But for her sake this vow I make,
  And solemnly I swear it,
That while I own a single crown
  She's welcome for to share it;
And my roguish boy his Mother's joy
  And the darling of his Pater,
For him I boast my pains and cost,
  Although a Fornicator.

Ye wenching blades whose hireling jades
  Have tipt you off blue-joram,
I tell you plain, I do disdain
  To rank you in the Quorum;
But a bony lass upon the grass
  To teach her esse Mater,
And no reward but fond regard,
  O that's a Fornicator.

Your warlike Kings and Heros bold,
  Great Captains and Commanders;
Your mighty Caesars fam'd of old,
  And conquering Alexanders;
In fields they fought and laurels bought,
  And bulwarks strong did batter,
But still they grac'd our noble list,
  And ranked Fornicator!!!

MY GIRL SHE'S AIRY

TUNE: *Black Joke*

∽◈∽

MS, from a transcript of the original holograph, sold at
Sotheby's, November 13, 1934. These verses, unknown to any
edition of *The Merry Muses*, were composed during Burns's
amour with Betty Paton, and were copied into his Common-
place Book in September, 1784. The following version was sent
to Robert Ainslie, July 29, 1787. [DLF]

∽◈∽

My Girl she's airy, she's buxom and gay,
Her breath is as sweet as the blossoms in May;
  A touch of her lips it ravishes quite;
She's always good natur'd, good humor'd and free;
She dances, she glances, she smiles with a glee;
  Her eyes are the lightenings of joy and delight;
Her slender neck, her handsome waist
Her hair well buckl'd, her stays well lac'd,
Her taper white leg, with an et, and a, c,
  For her a, b, e, d, and her c, u, n, t,
  And Oh, for the joys of a long winter night!!!!

THERE WAS TWA WIVES

Not in any edition of *The Merry Muses*. Scott Douglas printed
a garbled version of part of the first stanza. Burns sent the song
to Robert Cleghorn, probably in January, 1792 (DLF, *L* II,
103), with the following introduction:

> . . . I make you [a] present of the following new Edition
> of an old Cloaciniad song, [a] species of composition which I
> have heard you admire, and a kind of song which I know
> you wanted much.—It is sung to an old tune, something
> like Tak your auld cloak about you—.

This text is from a transcript, by the late Davidson Cook, of
a MS in the Honresfield collection. [DLF]

There was twa wives, and twa witty wives,
 As e'er play'd houghmagandie,
And they coost out, upon a time,
 Out o'er a drink o' brandy;
Up Maggy rose, and forth she goes,
 And she leaves auld Mary flytin,
And she f—rted by the byre-en'
 For she was gaun a sh—ten.

She f—rted by the byre-en'
 She f—rted by the stable;
And thick and nimble were her steps
 As fast as she was able:
Till at yon dyke-back the hurly brak,
 But raxin for some dockins,
The beans and pease eam down her thighs,
 And she cackit a' her stockins.

B. *Collected by Burns*

BROSE AN' BUTTER

This is the earliest surviving specimen of Burns's work as a collector of folksongs. The text is written on the reverse of his draft of a letter to Margaret Kennedy of Daljarrock (formerly in the Adam Collection, New York). That letter was composed either in 1786 or in the autumn of 1785, and the handwriting of the song proves that it is approximately contemporary with the letter. The second stanza of Burns's version does not appear in MMC, which has, however, a final stanza not in Burns's MS. The order of his stanzas differs also. [DLF]

Gie my Love brose, brose,
  Gie my Love brose an' butter;
An' gie my Love brose, brose,
  Yestreen he wanted his supper.

Jenny sits up i' the laft,
  Jocky wad fain a been at her;
There cam a win' out o' the wast
  Made a' the windows to clatter.

      Gie my Love brose &c.

A dow's a dainty dish;
  A goose is hollow within;
A sight wad mak you blush,
  But a' the fun's to fin'.

      Gie my &c.

My Dadie sent me to the hill,
  To pow my minnie some heather;

[71]

An' drive it in your fill,
Ye're welcome to the leather.
Gie my &c.

A mouse is a merry wee beast;
A modewurck wants the een;
An' O for the touch o' the thing
I had i' my nieve yestreen.
Gie my Love &c.

The lark she loves the grass;
The hen she loves the stibble;
An' hey for the Gar'ner lad,
To gully awa wi' his dibble.—

Extra final stanza from MMC:
We a' were fou yestreen,
The nicht shall be its brither;
And hey, for a roaring pin
To nail twa wames thegither!

In MMC lines 3 and 4 of the chorus read:
For nane in Carrick wi him
Can gie a c–t its supper.
[SGS]

CUMNOCK PSALMS

❧❧

MS, Morgan Library, New York. In September, 1794, Burns wrote to George Thomson (DLF, *L* II, 257):

> Do you know a droll Scots song more famous for its humor than delicacy, called, The grey goose & the gled?—Mr Clarke took down the notes, such as they are, at my request, which I shall give with some decenter verses to Johnson.—Mr. Clarke says that the tune is positively an old Chant of the ROMISH CHURCH; which corroborates the old tradition, that at the Reformation, the Reformers burlesqued much of the old Church Music with setting them to bawdy verses. As a further proof, the common name for this song is Cumnock Psalms.—As there can be no harm in transcribing a stanza of a Psalm, I shall give you two or three: possibly the song is new to you. (Printed in MMC) [DLF]

❧❧

As I looked o'er yon castle wa',
   I spied a grey goose & a gled;
They had a fecht between them twa,
   And O, as their twa hurdies gade.—

     Chorus

   With a hey ding it in, & a how ding it in,
     And a hey ding it in, it's lang to day:
   Tal larietal, tallarietal
     Tal larietal, tal larie tay.

         2

She strack up & he strack down.
   Between them twa they made a mowe,
And ilka fart that the carlin gae,
   It's four o' them wad fill a bowe.
            With a hey ding it in &c.

3

Temper your tail, Carlin, he cried,
   Temper your tail by Venus' law;
Double your dunts, the dame replied,
   Wha the deil can hinder the wind to blaw!
           With a hey &c.

4

For were ye in my saddle set,
   And were ye weel girt in my gear,
If the wind o' my arse blaw you out o' my cunt,
   Ye'll never be reckoned a man o' weir.—
           With a hey &c.

5

He placed his Jacob whare she did piss,
   And his ballocks whare the wind did blaw,
And he grippet her fast by the goosset o' the arse
   And he gae her cunt the common law.
           With a hey &c.

Burns to Thomson: "So much for the Psalmody of Cummock."
Thomson's appended comment: "Delicate psalmody indeed. G.T."
(DLF, *L* II, 257).

Stanzas 2 and 3 occur slightly changed as stanza 2 of "Wha the Deil
can hinder the Wind to blaw?" (see Section IV). Burns's "decenter
verses" are "As I stood by yon roofless tower" (HH III. 144). [SGS]

GREEN GROW THE RASHES O (A)

❧

This recension of an old Scots song was sent by Burns to John Richmond, September 3, 1786, with the note in which he announced that Jean Armour had just borne him twins (DLF, *L* I, 41). The MS was included in the Armour sale at the American Art Association–Anderson Galleries, New York, April 22, 1937; the present text is from the holograph, examined by courtesy of Mr. David A. Randall of Charles Scribner's Sons. [DLF]

❧

A Fragment—

Chorus

Green grow the rashes O,
Green grow the rashes O,
The lasses they hae wimble bores,
The widows they hae gashes O.

1

In sober hours I am a priest;
  A hero when I'm tipsey, O;
But I'm a king and ev'ry thing,
  When wi' a wanton Gipsey, O.

Green grow &c.

2

'Twas late yestreen I met wi' ane,
  An' wow, but she was gentle, O!
Ae han' she pat roun' my cravat,
  The tither to my p—— O.

Green grow &c.

I dought na speak—yet was na fley'd—
My heart play'd duntie, duntie, O;
An' ceremony laid aside,
I fairly fun' her c—ntie, O.—
Green grow &c.

—Multa desunt—

MMC has two versions. One (see Section II), which Scott Douglas in a penciled note attributes to Burns, is entirely different in its stanzas but has the chorus as above. The other which MMC describes as "An Older Edition" (i.e. version), consists of stanzas 2 and 3 as above, with lines 3 and 4 of the chorus as:

> The sweetest bed that e'er I got
> Was the bellies o' the lassies, O.

One or other or all of these versions inspired Burns's famous song of the same name (HH I, 251). [SGS]

MUIRLAND MEG

TUNE: *Saw ye my Eppie McNab?*

◦◈◦

Published in MMC, where it has a chorus:

> And for a sheep-cloot she'll do't, she'll do't,
> And for a sheep-cloot she'll do't;
> And for a toop-horn she'll do't to the morn,
> And merrily turn and do't, and do't.

M'Naught calls it "An old song." The following text, in
Burns's later hand, is copied, by permission, from a holograph
which in February, 1949, was in the possession of the Rosen-
bach Company, New York. It lacks the chorus. [DLF]
Attributed to Burns in Cunningham MS (GL, 136). [SGS]

◦◈◦

Among our young lassies there's Muirland Meg,
She'll beg or she work, & she'll play or she beg,
At thirteen her maidenhead flew to the gate,
And the door o' her cage stands open yet.—

Her kittle black een they wad thirl you thro'.
Her rose-bud lips cry, kiss me now;
The curls & links o' her bonie black hair,—
Wad put you in mind that the lassie has mair.—

An armfu' o' love is her bosom sae plump,
A span o' delight is her middle sae jimp;
A taper, white leg, & a thumpin thie,
And a fiddle near by, an ye play a wee!—

Love's her delight, & kissin's her treasure;
She'll stick at nae price, & ye gie her gude measure,
As lang's a sheep-fit, & as girt's a goose-egg,
And that's the measure o' Muirland Meg.

[77]

TODLEN HAME

(By David McCulloch of Ardwell, Galloway)

MS, formerly in the Bixby Collection, St. Louis. Printed in DLF, *L* II, 309. Not in any edition of *The Merry Muses*. Burns wrote from Dumfries, August 21, 1795, to his Crochallan crony Robert Cleghorn of Saughton Mills, Edinburgh, enclosing another bawdy song, which we have been unable to trace [SGS]:

> . . . Inclosed you have Clarke's Gaffer Gray.—I have not time [to make a] copy of it, so, when you have taken a copy for yourself, please return me the Original.—I need not caution you against giving copies to any other person.— "Peggy Ramsay," I shall expect to find in Gaffer Gray's company, when he returns to Dumfries.— . . . P.S. Did you ever meet with the following, Todlin hame—By the late Mr. McCulloch, of Ardwell—Galloway—

When wise Solomon was a young man o' might,
He was canty, & liked a lass ilka night;
But when he grew auld that he was na in trim,
He cried out, "In faith, Sirs! I doubt it's a sin!"

> Todlen hame, todlen hame,
> Sae round as a neep we gang todlen hame.—

But we're no come to that time o' life yet, ye ken;
The bottle's half-out—but we'll fill it again:
As for Solomon's doubts, wha the devil cares for't!
He's a damn'd churlish fallow that likes to spill sport.

> Todlen &c.

[78]

A bicker that's gizzen'd, it's nae worth a doit;
Keep it wat, it will haud in—it winna let out:
A chiel that's ay sober, is damn'd ill to ken;
Keep him wat wi' gude drink—& ye'll find him out
   then.—

   Todlen &c.

May our house be weel theekit, our pantry ay fu',
Wi' rowth in our cellar for weetin' our mou';
Wi a tight, caller hizzie, as keen as oursels,
Ay ready to souple *the whistle & bells!!!*

   Todlen hame &c.

WAP AND ROW

ᐤ◆ᐤ

This song was printed as No. 457 in Vol. v of *The Scots Musical Museum* to the tune of "The Reel o' Stumpie," and under that title was included in MMC, where it has three stanzas. The present text is taken from a holograph formerly in the Gribbel Collection, Philadelphia, where it was accompanied by the two prose memoranda which follow. [DLF]

ᐤ◆ᐤ

Chorus—(Note, the song begins with the Chorus)
>   Wap & row, wap & row,
>   Wap & row the feetie o't
>   I thought I was a maiden fair,
>   Till I heard the greetie o't.—

>   My daddie was a fiddler fine,
>   My minnie she made mantie, O,
>   And I myself a thumpin quine,
>   And try'd the rantie-tantie O.

>   Wap and row &c.

Tibbie Nairn's exclamation, coming in one Sunday evening from hearing Mr Whitefield—
  "G—d's mercy! No a c—ndum in this house for the gentle-men! God help me, what'll come o' this house when I'm in the arms o' the blessed Jesus!"—

Observation of a beggar woman in the Merse on a sturdy herd-lad giving her a—
  "God's blessin on you, my bairn! I hae haen mair flesh in my pot, but I canna say I had ever mair kail."—

The two other stanzas printed in MMC are interpolated between the chorus and stanza above:
>   Lang kail, pease and leeks,
>   They were at the kirst'nin' o't,

Lang lads wanton [i.e. wanting] breeks,
   They were at the getting o't.

The Bailie he gaed farthest ben,
   Mess John was ripe and ready o't;
But the Sherra had a wanton fling,
   The Sherra was the daddie o't.

[SGS]

THERE CAM A SOGER

MS, National Library of Scotland. On March 8, 1795, Burns
wrote to Patrick Miller, Jr., of Dalswinton (DLF, *L* II,
291): "When you return to the country, you will find us all
Sogers. This a propos, brings to my mind an old Scotish
stanza—" which he quotes as follows.

The verse is not in MMC, but an obviously garbled version of
it forms stanza 3 of "The Reels of Bogie" (see Section IV) as
printed in the 1827 edition. [DLF]

There cam a soger here to stay,
  He swore he wadna steer me;
But, lang before the break o' day,
  He cuddl'd muddl'd near me:
He set a stiff thing to my wame,
  I docht na bide the bends o't;
But lang before the grey morn cam,
  I soupl'd baith the ends o't.—

SING, UP WI'T, AILY

❖

MS, from a transcript of the original holograph sold at Sotheby's, November 13, 1934 (PMLA, L I, 4). This fragment, probably traditional, is included in a letter from Burns to Robert Ainslie, July 29, 1787. It is not in any edition of *The Merry Muses*. [DLF]

❖

Sing, Up wi't, Aily, Aily;
　Down wi' kimmerland jock;
Deil ram their lugs, quo' Willie,
　But I hae scour'd her dock!

Encore!

GREEN SLEEVES

❦

Probably traditional. The text is from a holograph in the Huntington Library, which has on its recto the song, "And I'll kiss thee yet, yet, . . . My bonie Peggy Alison." The lines are not in any edition of *The Merry Muses*; the music is not in Dick. A Jacobite version of the words was taken down by Boswell from Mrs Mackinnon of Corriechatachain. Its chorus is as the first stanza below (*Tour of the Hebrides*, 26 September, 1773). [DLF]

❦

> Green sleeves and tartan ties
> Mark my true love whare she lies:
> I'll be at her or she rise,
>   My fiddle and I thegither.
>
> Be it by the chrystal burn,
> Be it by the milkwhite thorn;
> I shall rouse her in the morn,
>   My fiddle and I thegither.

See also Ht. Hd. 177.

> Green sleeves and pudden-pyes,
> Come tell me where my true love lyes,
> And I'll be wi' her ere she rise:
>   Fidle a' the gither!
>
> Hey ho! and about she goes,
> She's milk in her breasts, she's none in her toes,
> She's a hole in her a—, you may put in your nose,
>   Sing: hey, boys, up go we!
>
> Green sleeves and yellow lace,
> Maids, maids, come, marry a pace!
> The batchelors are in a pitiful case
>   To fidle a' the gither.

[SGS]

II

⌒◇⌒

BY OR
ATTRIBUTED
TO BURNS
FROM PRINTED SOURCES

Notes in this section are by
SYDNEY GOODSIR SMITH
unless otherwise initialled

THE PATRIARCH

TUNE (in MMC): *The Auld Cripple Dow*

⌀⟡⌀

From MMC. A note by W. Scott Douglas in MMC holograph addenda reads: "Original MS [which we have been unable to trace—SGS] possessed by Mr. Roberts, Town-Clerk of Forfar. It is headed:

> 'A Wicked Song.
> 'Author's name unknown.
> 'Tune—The Waukin' o' a winter's night.

'The Publisher to the Reader,

'Courteous Reader,

'The following is certainly the production of one of those licentious, ungodly (too-much-abounding in this our day) wretches who take it as a compliment to be called wicked, providing you allow them to be witty. Pity it is that while so many tar-barrels in the country are empty, and so many gibbets untenanted, some example is not made of these profligates.'"

To which M'Naught (in M'N) adds: "Burns pursues this satirical-humorous vein in his mock manifesto as 'Poet-Laureat and Bard in Chief . . . of Kyle, Cuningham and Carrick,' addressed ['in the name of the NINE'] to William Chalmers and John M'Adam, 'Students and Practitioners in the ancient and mysterious Science of Confounding Right and Wrong.'"

"RIGHT TRUSTY [it runs]: Be it known, that . . . We have discovered a certain [bawdy], nefarious, abominable and wicked Song or Ballad, a copy whereof We have here inclosed; Our Will therefore is . . . the said copy . . . be consumed by fire [at the Cross of Ayr] . . . in the presence of all Beholders, in abhorrence of, and terrorem to, all such Compositions and Composers . . . Given at Mauchline this twentieth day of November, Anno Domini one thousand seven hundred and eighty-six. GOD SAVE THE BARD." (DLF, *L* I, 52)

As honest Jacob on a night,
  Wi' his beloved beauty,
Was duly laid on wedlock's bed,
  And noddin' at his duty.
                  Tal de dal &c.

"How lang, she says, ye fumblin' wretch,
  "Will ye be f—g at it?
"My eldest wean might die of age,
  "Before that ye could get it.

"Ye pegh and grane, and groazle there,
  "And mak an unco splutter,
"And I maun ly and thole you here,
  "And fient a hair the better."

Then he, in wrath, put up his graith,
  "The deevil's in the hizzie!
"I m—w you as I m—w the lave,
  "And night and day I'm bisy.

"I've bairn'd the servant gypsies baith,
  "Forbye your titty Leah;
"Ye barren jad, ye put me mad,
  "What mair can I do wi you.

"There's ne'er a m—w I've gi'en the lave,
  "But ye ha'e got a dizzen;
"An d—n'd a ane ye'se get again,
  "Although your c—t should gizzen."

Then Rachel calm, as ony lamb,
  She claps him on the waulies;
Quo' she, "ne'er fash a woman's clash,
  "In trowth ye m—w me braulies.

[88]

"My dear 'tis true, for mony a m—w,
  "I'm your ungratefu' debtor,
"But ance again, I dinna ken,
  "We'll aiblens happen better."

Then honest man! wi' little wark,
  He soon forgat his ire;
The patriarch, he coost the sark,
  And up and till't like fire!

THE BONNIEST LASS

From MM27, reprinted in M'N. Not in MMC. "Much in the vein of 'The Patriarch,'" says M'Naught. There is little room for doubt that this is by Burns. [JB, SGS]

◇

The bonniest lass that ye meet neist
　　Gie her a kiss an' a' that,
In spite o' ilka parish priest,
　　Repentin' stool, an' a' that.

　　　　For a' that an' a' that,
　　　　　　Their mim-mou'd sangs an' a' that,
　　　　In time and place convenient,
　　　　　　They'll do't themselves for a' that.

Your patriarchs in days o' yore,
　　Had their handmaids an' a' that;
O' bastard gets, some had a score
　　An' some had mair than a' that.

　　　　For a' that an' a' that,
　　　　　　Your langsyne saunts, an' a' that,
　　　　Were fonder o' a bonie lass,
　　　　　　Than you or I, for a' that.

King Davie, when he waxed auld,
　　An's bluid ran thin, an' a' that,
An' fand his cods were growin' cauld,
　　Could not refrain, for a' that.

　　　　For a' that an' a' that,
　　　　　　To keep him warm an' a' that,
　　　　The daughters o' Jerusalem
　　　　　　Were waled for him, an' a' that.

Wha wadna pity thae sweet dames
  He fumbled at, an' a' that,
An' raised their bluid up into flames
  He couldna drown, for a' that.

    For a' that an' a' that,
      He wanted pith, an' a' that;
    For, as to what we shall not name,
      What could he do but claw that.

King Solomon, prince o' divines,
  Wha proverbs made, an' a' that,
Baith mistresses an' concubines
  In hundreds had, for a' that.

    For a' that an' a' that,
      Tho' a preacher wise an' a' that,
    The smuttiest sang that e'er was sung
      His Sang o' Sangs is a' that.

Then still I swear, a clever chiel
  Should kiss a lass, an' a' that,
Tho' priests consign him to the deil,
  As reprobate, an' a' that.

    For a' that an' a' that,
      Their canting stuff, an' a' that,
    They ken nae mair wha's reprobate
      Than you or I, for a' that.

GODLY GIRZIE

TUNE: *Wat ye wha I met yestreen?*

●❖○

From MMC. Ascribed to Burns by Scott Douglas. M'Naught
says "Anonymous, but quite in Burns's style." DLF in MP
(XXX, I) writes:

"A holograph of 'Godly Girzie' is described in the *Burns
Chronicle*, III (1894), 142. It bears the caption, 'A new song—
from an old story': the quoted [first] stanza varies in a couple
of readings from the *Muses* text. M'Naught is silent about this
MS, which appears to confirm Burns's authorship."

According to the *Burns Chronicle's* description, the song is
written on the back of a page containing "Yestreen I had a
pint o' wine." In i, 3 "Kilmarnock" has been written in above
"The winnocks" [deleted].

●❖○

The night it was a haly night,
   The day had been a haly day;
Kilmarnock gleamed wi' candle light,
   As Girzie hameward took her way.
A man o' sin, ill may he thrive!
And never haly-meeting see!
Wi' godly Girzie met belyve,
   Amang the Cragie hills sae hie.

The chiel' was wight, the chiel' was stark,
   He wad na wait to chap nor ca',
And she was faint wi haly wark,
   She had na pith to say him na.
But ay she glowr'd up to the moon,
   And ay she sigh'd most piouslie;
"I trust my heart's in heaven aboon,
   "Whare'er your sinfu' p—e be."

WHA'LL MOW ME NOW?

TUNE: *Comin' thro' the rye*

◇

From MMC. Attributed to Burns by Hecht (*Archiv*); by DLF
(MP, xxx, i, Aug. 1932); by Aitken, who prints in part stanzas
i, ii, v, vi, in *Ald* 1893 (IIII, 75); and by Scott Douglas in a
pencilled note in MMC, "An old song," says M'Naught.

◇

O, I hae tint my rosy cheek,
    Likewise my waste sae sma';
O wae gae by the sodger lown,
    The sodger did it a'.

    O wha'll m—w me now, my jo,
      An' wha'll m—w me now:
    A sodger wi' his bandileers
      Has bang'd my belly fu'.

Now I maun thole the scornfu' sneer
    O' mony a saucy quine;
When, curse upon her godly face!
    Her c—t's as merry's mine.

Our dame hauds up her wanton tail,
    As due as she gaes lie;
An' yet misca's [a] young thing,
    The trade if she but try.

Our dame can lae her ain gudeman,
    An' m—w for glutton greed;
An' yet misca' a poor thing,
    That's m—n' for its bread.

Alake! sae sweet a tree as love,
　Sic bitter fruit should bear!
Alake, that e'er a merry a—e,
　Should draw a sa'tty tear.

But deevil damn the lousy loon,
　Denies the bairn he got!
Or lea's the merry a—e he lo'ed,
　To wear a ragged coat!

On the last stanza, DLF (*op. cit.*) writes, and JB and SGS concur, that "One is bound to agree with Professor Hecht and other critics in holding that Burns never wrote a more characteristic stanza than the closing one."

HAD I THE WYTE SHE BADE ME (A)

TUNE: *Highland Hills*

❤

From MMC. "The inference is irresistible," say Henley and
Henderson (III, 411), "that the fragment in the Herd MS [see
Section III] suggested two songs to Burns: one for publication
[HH, III, 149], the other—*not*." Hecht (*op. cit.*) considers this
"variant in the *Merry Muses* probably composed by Burns,"
and later, in comparing the Herd and *Muses* versions, says,
"There is no doubt whatever that Burns himself was the
author of the changes," and with this verdict JB and SGS
entirely agree. Scott Douglas in a penciled note in MMC says
"Old with retouching" and M'Naught "An old song."
Attributed to Burns in Cunningham MS (GL, 135).

❤

Had I the wyte, had I the wyte,
   Had I the wyte she bad me;
For she was steward in the house,
   And I was fit-man laddie;
And when I wadna do't again,
   A silly cow * she ca'd me;
She straik't my head, and clapt my cheeks,
   And lous'd my breeks and bad me.

Could I for shame, could I for shame,
   Could I for shame deny['d] her;
Or in the bed was I to blame,
   She bad me lye beside her:
I pat six inches in her wame,
   A quarter wadna fly'd her;
For ay the mair I ca'd it hame,
   Her ports they grew the wider.

* "*coof*" in Cunningham MS.

[95]

My tartan plaid, when it was dark,
   Could I refuse to share it;
She lifted up her holland-sark,
   And bad me fin' the gair o't:
Or how could I amang the garse,
   But gie her hilt and hair o't;
She clasped her houghs about my a—e,
   And ay she glowr'd for mair o't.

DAINTY DAVIE (A)

From MMC. Considered by Hecht (*op. cit.*) to be Burns's own version of the old song (see Section III and footnote). Attributed to Burns in Cunningham MS (GL, 134).

Being pursu'd by the dragoons,
    Within my bed he was laid down
And weel I wat he was worth his room,
    My ain dear dainty Davie.

        O leeze me on * his curly pow,
        Bonie Davie, dainty Davie;
        Leeze me on his curly pow,
        He was my dainty Davie.

My minnie laid him at my back,
    I trow he lay na lang at that,
But turn'd, and in a verra crack
    Produc'd a dainty Davie.

Then in the field amang the pease,
    Behin' the house o' Cherrytrees,
Again he wan atweesh my thies,
    And, splash! gaed out his gravy.

But had I goud, or had I land,
    It should be a' at his command;
I'll ne'er forget what he pat i' my hand,
    It was a dainty Davie.

* See footnote, p. 60.

JB and SGS share Hecht's opinion when he writes in *Archiv;* "Herd's first verse [see Section III] is missing in MMC. The third is enlarged to two verses which for reasons of gradation and development of the episode are transferred to the beginning of the poem. The rhyme 'gravy' instead of Herd's regularly repeated 'Davie' [in this regard, see also "The Tailor cam to clout the claes" in Section III] may be taken as an indication that the verse was not in the original version. Noteworthy also is the desire to make clearer the allusion to the proper name Cherrytrees (also in the third verse) which is hardly recognizable in Herd's version. The fourth verse with the strong beginning of lines 1 and 2 is missing in Herd. The comparison makes it clear that the version of Dainty Davie in MMC was derived from the version given by Herd with express artistic intentions. There is no doubt whatever that Burns himself was the author of these changes. This supports our conjecture that even in the cases in which we have no other versions apart from those in MMC the gist of the song may be old but very frequently it underwent the poet's encroachment to heighten the artistic effect."

THE TROGGER

TUNE: *Gillicrankie*

❦

From MMC. "May very well be from Burns" (HH III, 415)—it has our vote (JB, SGS). Attributed to Burns "certainly" by Scott Douglas in a pencilled note in MMC. Described by M'Naught as "anonymous—probably not older than Burns's time." 1964: the Cunningham MS proves that this is definitely by Burns (GL, 136).

❦

As I cam down by Annan side,
　　Intending for the border,
Amang the Scroggie banks and braes
　　Wha met I but a trogger.
He laid me down upon my back,
　　I thought he was but jokin',
Till he was in me to the hilts,
　　O the deevil tak sic troggin!

What could I say, what could I do,
　　I bann'd and sair misca'd him,
But whiltie-whaltie gaed his a—e,
　　The mair that I forbade him:
He stell'd his foot against a stane,
　　And double'd ilka stroke in,
Till I gaed daft amang his hands,
　　O the deevil tak sic troggin!

Then up we raise, and took the road,
　　And in by Ecclefechan,
Where the brandy-stoup we gart it clink,
　　And the strang-beer ream the quech in.
Bedown the bents o' Bonshaw braes,
　　We took the partin' yokin';
But I've claw'd a sairy c—t sinsyne,
　　O the deevil tak sic troggin!

PUT BUTTER IN MY DONALD'S BROSE

❧

From MMC, where it is entitled "For a' that and a' that."
Attributed to Burns by Henley and Henderson (HH II, 304).
Burns used the first two lines of the refrain for the Bard's Song
and the Sailor's Song in "The Jolly Beggars" (HH II, 1) and in
"Is there for Honest Poverty" (HH III, 271). He wrote to
Thomson, August 3, 1795 (DLF, L II, 307): "I inclose you a
'For a' that & a' that' which was never in print: it is a much
superiour song to mine—I have been told that it was composed
by a lady—."

❧

Put butter in my Donald's brose,
   For weel does Donald fa' that;
I loe my Donald's tartans weel
   His naked a—e and a' that.

     For a' that, and a' that,
       And twice as meikle's a' that,
     The lassie gat a skelpit doup,
       But wan the day for a' that.

For Donald swore a solemn aith,
   By his first hairy gravat!
That he wad fight the battle there,
   And stick the lass, and a' that.

His hairy b—s, side and wide,
   Hang like a beggar's wallet;
A p—e like a roaring-pin,
   She nicher'd when she saw that!!!

Then she turn'd up her hairy c—t,
   And she bade Donald claw that;
The deevil's dizzen Donald drew,
   And Donald gied her a' that.

HERE'S HIS HEALTH IN WATER

TUNE: *The job o' journey wark* (says SD)

✧

From MMC. Composed by Burns in 1786. Stanza i appeared in
SMM 1796 (v. 494) and most editions subsequently.

✧

Altho' my back be at the wa,
    An' tho' he be the fau'tor;
Altho' my back be at the wa',
    I'll drink his health in water.
O wae gae by his wanton sides,
    Sae brawly's he cou'd flatter.
I for his sake am slighted sair,
    An' dree the kintra clatter;
But let them say whate'er they like,
    Yet, here's his health in water.

He follow'd me baith out an' in,
    Thro' a' the nooks o' Killie;
He follow'd me baith out an' in,
    Wi' a stiff stanin' p-llie.
But when he gat atween my legs,
    We made an unco splatter;
An' haith, I trow, I soupled it,
    Tho' bauldly he did blatter;
But now my back is at the wa',
    Yet here's his health in water.

i, 7. MMC misprints I for his sake I'm . . .
i, 8. MMC misprints An' drees . . .

THE JOLLY GAUGER

TUNE: *We'll gang nae mair a rovin'*

◦◈◦

From MMC. Parody, "claimed for a fellow-exciseman" (HH
II, 297), of *The Jolly Beggar*, traditionally attributed to King
James V. DLF considers it might be by Burns: "If not . . .
original with Burns . . . probably touched up by him"
(MP xxx, 1). Attributed to Burns by Scott Douglas in a
pencilled note in MMC. It has obviously been written round the
"Observation of a beggar woman in the Merse" which Burns
took the trouble to preserve in the MS of "Wap and Row"
(Section I).

◦◈◦

There was a jolly gauger, a gauging he did ride,
And he has met a beggar down by yon river side.

An weel gang nae mair a rovin' wi' ladies to the wine,
When a beggar wi' her meal-pocks can fidge her tail
sae fine.

Amang the broom he laid her; amang the broom sae
green,
And he's fa'n to the beggar, as she had been a queen.
And we'll gang &c.

My blessings on thee, laddie, thou's done my turn sae
weel,
Wilt thou accept, dear laddie, my pock and pickle
meal?
And weel, &c.

Sae blyth the beggar took the bent, like ony bird in
spring,
Sae blyth the beggar took the bent, and merrily did
sing.
And weel, &c.

My blessings on the gauger, o' gaugers he's the chief,
Sic kail ne'er crost my kettle, nor sic a joint o'beef.
And weel, &c.

O GAT YE ME WI NAETHING?

TUNE: *Jacky Latin*

❖

From MMC. Origin of Burns's song "The Lass o' Ecclefechan"
(HH III, 156). Attributed to Burns by Henley and Henderson
(III, 415); by Scott Douglas in a pencilled note in MMC; and in
MM27. Might quite well be by Burns on the basis of an old
fragment, probably the first two lines.

❖

Gat ye me, O gat ye me,
  An' gat ye me wi' naething?
A rock, a reel, a spinning wheel,
  A gude black c—t was ae thing.
A tocher fine, o'er muckle far,
  When sic a scullion gat it;
Indeed, o'er muckle far, gudewife,
  For that was ay the fau't o't.

But had your tongue now, Luckie Lang,
  O had your tongue and jander,
I held the gate till you I met,
  Syne I began to wander;
I tint my whistle an' my sang,
  I tint my peace an' pleasure,
But your green grave now, Luckie Lang,
  Wad airt me to my treasure.

GIE THE LASS HER FAIRIN'

TUNE: *Cauld kail in Aberdeen*

ᴏ❖ᴏ

From MMC. Attributed to Burns in MM27 and by Scott
Douglas in a pencilled note in MMC. Quite likely too; the tune
was one of his favourites.

ᴏ❖ᴏ

O gie the lass her fairin' lad,
  O gie the lass her fairin',
An' something else she'll gie to you,
  That's waly worth the wearin';
Syne coup her o'er amang the creels,
  When ye hae taen your brandy,
The mair she bangs the less she squeels,
  An' hey for houghmagandie.

Then gie the lass a fairin', lad,
  O gie the lass her fairin',
And she'll gie you a hairy thing,
  An' of it be na sparin';
But coup her o'er amang the creels,
  An' bar the door wi' baith your heels,
The mair she bangs the less she squeels,
  An' hey for houghmagandie.

GREEN GROW THE RASHES (B)

ᗢ❖ᗡ

From MMC, where it is ascribed to Burns by Scott Douglas in a pencilled note. Burns wrote to George Thomson in April, 1793: "At any rate, my other Song 'Green grow the Rashes' will never suit.—That Song is current in Scotld under the old title, & sung to the merry old tune of that name; which of course would mar the progress of your Song to celebrity" (DLF, *L* II, 162). See also Section I.

ᗢ❖ᗡ

O wat ye ought o' fisher Meg,
  And how she trow'd the webster, O,
She loot me see her carrot c—t,
  And sell'd it for a labster, O.

Green grow the rashes, O,
  Green grow the rashes, O,
The lassies they hae wimble-bores,
  The widows they hae gashes, O.

Mistress Mary cow'd her thing,
  Because she wad be gentle, O,
And span the fleece upon a rock,
  To waft a Highland mantle, O.

An' heard ye o' the coat o' arms,
  The Lyon brought our lady, O,
The crest was, couchant, sable c—t,
  The motto—"*ready, ready*," O.

An' ken ye Leezie Lundie, O.
  The godly Leezie Lundie, O,
She m—s like reek thro' a' the week,
  But finger f—s on Sunday, O.

[105]

TAIL TODLE

TUNE: *Chevalier's Muster-Roll* (says SD)

ᗡᐧᗡ

From MMC, where it is attributed to Burns by Scott Douglas
in a pencilled note. There are versions of this still extant. Burns
might have tidied it up a bit when he came to write it down,
but probably not much more than that.

ᗡᐧᗡ

Our gudewife held o'er to Fife,
    For to buy a coal-riddle;
Lang or she came back again,
    Tammie gart my tail todle.

        Tail todle, tail todle;
        Tammie gart my tail todle;
        At my a—e wi' diddle doddle,
        Tammie gart my tail todle.

When I'm dead I'm out o' date;
    When I'm sick I'm fu' o' trouble;
When I'm weel I step about,
    An' Tammie gars my tail todle.

Jenny Jack she gae a plack,
    Helen Wallace gae a boddle,
Quo' the bride, it's o'er little
    For to mend a broken doddle.

I REDE YOU BEWARE O' THE RIPPLES

TUNE: *The Taylor's faun thro the bed*

ᐁ◈ᐁ

From MMC. Original of Burns's song "The Bonnie Moor Hen" (HH IV, 20) which Clarinda advised him not to publish "for your sake and mine," in a letter dated January 30, 1788. In MMC, Scott Douglas, in a pencilled note, attributes this version to Burns, as do Henley and Henderson (HH IV, 89).

ᐁ◈ᐁ

I rede you beware o' the ripples, young man,
I rede you beware o' the ripples, young man;
Tho' the saddle be saft, ye needna ride aft,
For fear that the girdin' beguile ye, young man.

I rede you beware o' the ripples, young man,
I rede you beware o' the ripples, young man;
Tho' music be pleasure, tak' music in measure,
Or ye may want win' i' your whistle, young man.

I rede you beware o' the ripples, young man,
I rede you beware o' the ripples, young man;
Whate'er ye bestow, do less than ye dow,
The mair will be thought o' your kindness, young man.

I rede you beware o' the ripples, young man,
I rede you beware o' the ripples, young man;
Gif you wad be strang, and wish to live lang,
Dance less wi' your a—e to the kipples, young man.

OUR JOHN'S BRAK YESTREEN

TUNE: *Gramachree*

◦◈◦

From MMC, where it is attributed to Burns by Scott Douglas
in a pencilled note.

◦◈◦

Twa neebor wives sat i' the sun,
    A twynin' at their rocks,
An' they an argument began,
    An' a' the plea was c—ks.

'Twas whether they were sinnens strang,
    Or whether they were bane?
An' how they row'd about your thumb,
    And how they stan't themlane?

First, Raichie gae her rock a rug,
    An' syne she claw'd her tail;
"When our Tam draws on his breeks,
    "It waigles like a flail."

Says Bess, "they're bane I will maintain,
    "And proof in han' I'll gie;
"For our John's it brak yestreen,
    "And the margh ran down my thie."

GRIZZEL GRIMME

∽◈∾

By Burns. From HH (ii, 459): ". . . Inscribed by Burns in a
volume of the *Glenriddell Collections*. . . . The epitaph is thus
prefaced: 'Passing lately through Dunblane, while I stopped
to refresh my horse, the following ludicrous epitaph, which I
picked up from an old tombstone among the ruins of the
ancient Abbey, struck me particularly, being myself a native
of Dumfriesshire.' The common version of the last two lines is
this: 'O Death, thou surely art not nice To lie with sic a
bitch.'" Not in any edition of *The Merry Muses*.

∽◈∾

Grim Grizzel was a mighty Dame
　Weel kend on Cluden-side:
Grim Grizzel was a mighty Dame
　O' meikle fame and pride.

When gentles met in gentle bowers
　And nobles in the ha',
Grim Grizzle was a mighty Dame,
　The loudest o' them a'.

Where lawless Riot rag'd the night
　And Beauty durst na gang,
Grim Grizzel was a mighty Dame
　Wham nae man e'er wad wrang.

Nor had Grim Grizzel skill alane
　What bower and ha' require;
But she had skill, and meikle skill,
　In barn and eke in byre.

Ae day Grim Grizzel walkèd forth,
　As she was wont to do,
Alang the banks o' Cluden fair,
　Her cattle for to view.

The cattle sh— o'er hill and dale
    As cattle will incline,
And sair it grieved Grim Grizzel's heart
    Sae muckle muck tae tine.

And she has ca'd on John o' Clods,
    Of her herdsmén the chief,
And she has ca'd on John o' Clods,
    And tell'd him a' her grief:—

"Now wae betide thee, John o' Clods!
    I gie thee meal and fee,
And yet sae meickle muck ye tine
    Might a' be gear to me!

"Ye claut my byre, ye sweep my byre,
    The like was never seen;
The very chamber I lie in
    Was never half sae clean.

"Ye ca' my kye adown the loan
    And there they a' discharge:
My Tammie's hat, wig, head and a'
    Was never half sae large!

"But mind my words now, John o' Clods,
    And tent me what I say:
My kye shall sh— ere they gae out,
    That shall they ilka day.

"And mind my words now, John o' Clods,
    And tent now wha ye serve;
Or back ye'se to the Colonel gang,
    Either to steal or starve."

Then John o' Clods, he lookèd up
   And syne he lookèd down;
He lookèd east, he lookèd west,
   He lookèd roun' and roun'.

His bonnet and his rowantree club
   Frae either hand did fa';
Wi' lifted een and open mouth
   He naething said at a'.

At length he found his trembling tongue,
   Within his mouth was fauld:—
"Ae silly word frae me, madám,
   Gin I daur be sae bauld.

"Your kye will at nae bidding sh—,
   Let me do what I can;
Your kye will at nae bidding sh—,
   Of onie earthly man.

"Tho' ye are great Lady Glaur-hole,
   For a' your power and art
Tho' ye are great Lady Glaur-hole,
   They winna let a fart."

"Now wae betide thee, John o' Clods!
   An ill death may ye die!
My kye shall at my bidding sh—,
   And that ye soon shall see."

Then she's ta'en Hawkie by the tail,
   And wrung wi' might and main,
Till Hawkie rowted through the woods
   Wi' agonising pain.

"Sh—, sh—, ye bitch," Grim Grizzel roar'd,
Till hill and valley rang;
"And sh—, ye bitch," the echoes roar'd
Lincluden wa's amang.

TWO EPITAPHS

⌖

From *The Court of Equity,* An Episode in the Life of Burns, Printed for Private Circulation, Edinburgh, 1910. See also *B.Chr.* 1902 (109). Not in any edition of *The Merry Muses.*

JOHANNES FUSCUS [JOHN BROWN]

HIC JACET

QUONDAM HOROLOGIORUM FABER IN M[AUCHLINE]

⌖

Lament him, M[auchline] husbands a',
　He aften did assist ye!
Tho ye had bidden years awa
　Your wives [wad] ne'er hae miss't ye.

Ye M[auchline] bairns, as bye ye pass
　To school in bands thegither,
O tread but lightly on the grass,
　Perhaps he was your father!

EPITAPH FOR

H[UGH] L[OGAN], ESQ., OF L[AIGHT]

⌖

Here lyes Squire Hugh—ye harlot crew,
　Come mak' your water on him,
I'm sure that he weel pleas'd would be
　To think ye pish'd upon him.

III

⌖

OLD SONGS
USED BY BURNS
FOR
POLITE VERSIONS

Notes in this section are by
SYDNEY GOODSIR SMITH
unless otherwise initialled

HAD I THE WYTE? (B)

❧

From Ht.Hd. (117). Hecht writes: "The fragment suggested Burns's 'Had I the Wyte' [HH III, 149] and a less delicate piece in *The Merry Muses*" (see Section II).

❧

Had I the wyte? had I the wyte?
Had I the wyte? She bad me,
And ay she gied me cheese and bread
To kiss her when she bad me,
For she was stewart in the house,
And I was footman-ladie,
And ay she gied me cheese and bread *
To kiss her, when she bad me.

* Sir Walter Scott's marginal note in Herd's MS:
    "For the two last lines read
      "And when I could na do't again:
      Silly loon she ca'd me."
Scott had borrowed Herd's MSS while compiling his *Minstrelsy of the Scottish Border,* as he acknowledges in his Introduction.

DAINTY DAVIE (B)

❧❖❧

From Ht.Hd. (140) and DH 1776 (ii, 215). Herd's note reads: "The following song was made upon Mess David Williamson on his getting with child the Lady Cherrytree's daughter, while the soldiers were searching the house to apprehend him for a rebel." This is the older version; the other, attributed to Burns, will be found in Section ii together with Hecht's comparison of the two. The chorus gave rise to Burns's song "Now Rosy May" (HH iii, 245). Burns's note in the Interleaved Copy of SMM reads: "The original verses of Dainty Davie and the anecdote which gave rise to them, are still extant, and were their delicacy equal to their humour, they would merit a place in any collection" (JCD, *N* 12). Not in any edition of *The Merry Muses*.

❧❖❧

It was in and through the window broads,
And all the tirliewirlies o'd:
The sweetest kiss that e'er I got
Was from my Dainty Davie.

    O leeze me on * your curly pow,
    Dainty Davie, dainty Davie,
    Leeze me on your curly pow,
    Mine ain dainty Davie.

It was down amang my daddy's pease,
And underneath the cherry-trees:
O there he kist me as he pleas'd,
For he was mine ain dear Davie.

When he was chased by a dragoon,
Into my bed he was laid down,
I thought him wordy o' his room,
And he's ay my dainty Davie.

* See footnote, p. 58.

[118]

LET ME IN THIS AE NIGHT

⌒◈⌒

From Ht.Hd. (149); also in DH 1776 (II, 167). Original of
Burns's song of same name (HH III, 274). Not printed in any
edition of *The Merry Muses*.

⌒◈⌒

O lassie, art thou sleeping yet,
Or are you waking, I wou'd wit?
For love has bound me hand and foot,
And I woul'd fain be in, jo.

O let me in this ae night, this ae, ae, ae night,
O let me in this ae night, and I'll ne'er come back
again, jo.

The morn it is the term-day,
I maun away, I canna stay:
O pity me, before I gae,
And rise and let me in, jo.

O let me in this ae night, this ae, ae, ae night,
O let me in this ae night, and I'll ne'er come back
again, jo.

The night it is baith cauld and weet,
The morn it will be snaw and sleet,
My shoen are frozen to my feet
Wi' standing on the plain, jo.

O let me in this ae night, this ae, ae, ae night,
O let me in this ae night, and I'll ne'er come back
again, jo.

I am the laird of windy-was,
I come na here without a cause,
And I hae gotten mony fa's
Upon a naked wame o!

O let me in this ae night, this ae, ae, ae night,
O let me in this ae night, and I'll ne'er come back
again, jo.

My father's wa'king on the street,
My mither the chamber-keys does keep,
My chamber-door does chirp and cheep,
And I dare nae let you in, jo!

O gae your way this ae night, this ae, ae, ae night
O gae your way this ae night, for I dare nae let you
in, jo!

But I'll come stealing saftly in
And cannily make little dinn,
And then the gate to you I'll find,
If you'l but direct me in, jo!

O let me in this ae night, this ae, ae, ae night,
O let me in this ae night, and I'll ne'er come back
again, jo.

Cast aff the shoen frae aff your feet,
Cast back the door up to the weet,
Syne into my bed you may creep
And do the thing you ken, jo.

O well's on me this ae night, this ae, ae, ae night,
O well's on me this ae night, that ere I let you in, jo!

She let him in sae cannily,
She let him in sae privily,
She let him in sae cannily,
To do the thing ye ken, jo.

O well's on me this ae night, this ae, ae, ae night,
O well's on me this ae night, that ere I let you in, jo!

But ere a' was done and a' was said,
Out fell the bottom of the bed,
The lassie lost her maidenhead,
And her mither heard the din, jo.

O the devil take this ae night, this ae, ae, ae night,
O the devil take this ae night, that ere I let ye in, jo!

In Herd's MS the choruses for ii, iii, iv, and vi, are merely indicated by
"O let &c,"

Chorus 5. DH 1776 . . . ways . . .
Chorus 7. *Ibid.*   O well's me on . . .

THE TAILOR

⸎

From DH 1769 (318) and MM27. Not in MMC. Suggested
Burns's song "The Tailor he came here to sew" (HH III, 179,
432). This text is Herd's except for each line 5 in stanzas
iv–ix which are taken from MM27; in Herd's text, line 5
repeats line 3 throughout.

⸎

The tailor came to clout the claise,
    Sic a braw fellow,
He filled the house a' fou o' fleas,
    Daffin down, and daffin down,
He filled the house a 'fou o' fleas,
    Daffin down and dilly.

The lassie slept ayont the fire,
    Sic a braw hissey!
Oh! she was a' his heart's desire,
    Daffin down, and daffin down,
Oh! she was a' his heart's desire,
    Daffin down and dilly.

The lassie she fell fast asleep,
    Sic a braw hissey!
The tailor close to her did creep,
    Daffin down, and daffin down,
The tailor close to her did creep,
    Daffin down and dilly.

The lassie waken'd in a fright,
    Sic a braw hissey!
Her maidenhead had taen the flight,
    Daffin down, and daffin down,
A tailor's bodkin caused the flight,
    Daffin down and dilly.

She sought it butt, she sought it ben,
  Sic a braw hissey!
And in beneath the clocken-hen,
  Daffin down, and daffin down,
It wasna but, it wasna ben,
  Daffin down and dilly.

She sought it in the owsen-staw,
  Sic a braw hissey!
Na, faith, quo' she, it's quite awa',
  Daffin down, and daffin down,
The tailor loon has stown't awa',
  Daffin down and dilly.

She sought it 'yont the knocking-stane,
  Sic a braw hissey!
Some day, quo' she, 'twill gang its lane,
  Daffin down, and daffin down,
For my tirly-wirly mak's its mane,
  Daffin down and dilly.

She ca'd the tailor to the court,
  Sic a braw hissey!
And a' the young men round about,
  Daffin down, and daffin down,
To gar the tailor mend her clout,
  Daffin down and dilly.

She gart the tailor pay a fine,
  Sic a braw hissey!
Gi'e me my maidenhead agen;
  Daffin down, and daffin down,
I'll hae my maidenhead again,
  Daffin down and dilly.

O what way wad ye hae't agen?
  Sic a braw hissey!
Oh! just the way that it was taen,
  Daffin down, and daffin down,
Come, just the way that it was ta'en,
  Daffin down and dilly.

EPPIE McNAB

❖

From *The Giblet Pye* (*c.* 1806). Not in any edition of the *Merry Muses*. Origin of Burns's song of same name (HH III, 101). Another version in Ht.Hd. (113). Burns's note in the Interleaved Copy of SMM: "The old song with this title, has more wit than decency" (JCD.*N* 58).

❖

O saw ye my Eppie McNab, McNab?
O saw ye my Eppie McNab, McNab?
She's down i' the yeard, she's kissen the laird,
As whilom's wi' honest Jock Rob, Jock Rob.

My blessings upo' thee, Jock Rob, Jock Rob,
My blessings upo' thee, Jock Rob, Jock Rob,
For in my gavel ye drive sic a dool,
Gard a' my buttocks play bab, bab, bab.

When first I met wi' thee, Jock Rob, Jock Rob,
When first I met wi' thee, Jock Rob, Jock Rob!
Thy breeks they were hol'd, and thy — hung out,
And thy — play'd ay did dod, did dod.

When first I met Eppie McNab, McNab,
I met wi' Eppie McNab, McNab;
Thy wee bit dud sark it play'd dod o' thy dab,
And thy — was as black as a crab, a crab.

DUNCAN GRAY

From MMC. Another version in Ht.Hd. (208). Basis of two of Burns's songs in Scots of same name (HH III, 23, 215), and one in English entitled "Let not women e'er complain" (HH III, 219). Of this last one Burns wrote significantly to Thomson on October 19, 1794:

> These English songs gravel me to death.—I have not that command of the language that I have of my native tongue. —In fact, I think my ideas are more barren in English than in Scottish.—I have been at "Duncan Gray" to dress it in English, but all I can do is deplorably stupid. (DLF, L II, 268).

Henley & Henderson (III, 452) and also Hecht (Ht.Hd. 319) consider Burns used Herd's MSS when collecting material for the *Scots Musical Museum* and that this version of "Duncan Gray" has been touched up by the bard in transcribing. The variations in Herd are given in the footnotes below. Examination of these will show that a literary hand (and whose but Burns's?) has been tidying up the cruder parts of the original. Herd has an extra final stanza. Attributed to Burns in Cunningham MS (GL, 138).

Can ye play me Duncan Gray,
  Ha, ha, the girdin' o't;
O'er the hills an' far awa,
  Ha, ha, ha, the girdin' o't,
Duncan came our Meg to woo,
Meg was nice an' wadna do,
But like an ither puff'd an' blew
  At offer o' the girdin' o't.

Duncan, he cam here again,
  Ha, ha, the girdin' o't,

A' was out, an' Meg her lane,
 Ha, ha, ha, the girdin' o't;
He kiss'd her butt, he kiss'd her ben,
He bang'd a thing against her wame;
But, troth, I now forget its name,
 But, I trow, she gat the girdin' o't.

She took him to the cellar then,
 Ha, ha, the girdin' o't,
To see gif he could do't again,
 Ha, ha, ha, the girdin' o't;
He kiss'd her ance, he kiss'd her twice,
An' by the bye he kiss'd her thrice
Till deil a mair the thing wad rise
 To gie her the long girdin' o't.

But Duncan took her to his wife,
 Ha, ha, the girdin' o't,
To be the comfort o' his life,
 Ha, ha, ha, the girdin' o't;
An' now she scauls baith night an' day,
Except when Duncan's at the play;
An' that's as seldom as he may,
 He's weary o'the girdin' o't.

i, 2, 4.	Ht.Hd.	The refrain is "High, hey the girdin' o't" throughout.
i, 5–8.	*Ibid.*	Duncan he came here to woo On a day when we were fou' And Meg she swore that she wou'd spew, If he gaed her the girdin o't.
i, 7.		An ither = an ether, adder.
ii, 1.	*Ibid.*	But Duncan he came here again
ii, 3.	*Ibid.*	And a' was out, but Meg her lane.
ii, 7.	*Ibid.*	But trouth I now forgot its name.
iii, 5–8.	*Ibid.*	He kiss'd her twice, he kiss'd her thrice, Till deil amair the thing wou'd rise Although she cried out baith her eyes To get the lang girdin o't.

iv, 5–8. *Ibid.*   But she scolds away both night and day
                    Without that Duncan still wou'd play,
                    And ay she cries: "Fy, Duncan Gray,
                        Come gae me the girdin o't."

Extra fifth stanza from Ht.Hd. (208):

He brought his wife a peck of malt,
    High, hey the girdin o't,
And bade her brew good swats o' that,
    High, hey the girdin o't,
She brew'd it thick, she mask'd it thin,
She threw the tap, but nane wou'd run,
Till Duncan he slipt in his pin,
    And then she got the girdin o't.

LOGAN WATER

◦◈◦

From MMC. Origin of Burns's song of same name (HH III, 262.)
He wrote to Thomson on April 7, 1793: "I remember two
ending lines of a verse in some of the old Songs of 'Logan
Water' (for I know a good many different ones) which I think
pretty—

> "Now my dear lad maun face his faes,
> Far far frae me & Logan braes!'"

Also in DH 1776 (II, 230) and Ht.Hd. (116); the variations here
are most probably improvements made by Burns in trans-
cribing.

◦◈◦

The Logan burn, the Logan braes,
I helped a bonie lassie on wi' her claes;
First wi' her stockings an' syne wi' her shoon,
But she gied me the glaiks when a' was done.

But an I had kend, what I ken now,
I wad a bang'd her belly fu';
Her belly fu' and her apron up,
An' shew'd her the road to the Logan kirk.

i, 1. DH   Logan water and Logan braes
i, 2. *Ibid.*   . . . claiths; Ht.Hd. . . . claes
i, 3. DH   . . . and then . . .
i, 4. *Ibid.*   And she gave me . . .
ii, 1. *Ibid.*   Omits "an"
ii, 2. *Ibid.*   I should have bang'd . . . fou
ii, 4. *Ibid.*   And hae shew'd her the way to Logan-kirk.

THE MILL MILL-O

From MMC. Origin of "The Soldier's Return" (HH iii, 212), by way of Allan Ramsay's "Beneath a green shade . . ." (TTM 1724), 153. Herd has a version (Ht.Hd. 115) but this is much superior poetically and has obviously felt the touch of Burns's hand. Burns wrote to Thomson, April 7, 1793: "The original song, 'The Mill mill O' though excellent, is, on account of decency, inadmissible."

As I came down yon water side
  And by yon Shillin hill, O;
There I spied a bonny lass,
  A lass that I loed right weel, O.

  The mill, mill, O, and the kill, kill, O,
    An' the coggin' o' Peggy's wheel, O,
  The sack an' the sieve, a' she did leave,
    An' danc'd the millars reel, O.

I spier'd at her, gin she cou'd play,
  But the lassie had nae skill, O;
An' yet she was nae a' to blame,
  She pat it in my will, O.

Then she fell o'er, an' sae did I,
  And danc'd the millars reel, O,
Whene'er that bonny lassie comes again,
  She shall hae her ma't ground weel, O.

i, 1.	Ht.Hd.	. . . came up yon . . .
i, 2.	*Ibid.*	And down yon . . .;
i, 3.	*Ibid.*	There I did spy . . .
i, 4.	*Ibid.*	A lass I loo'd . . .
ii, 1.	*Ibid.*	I asked her if she could play
ii, 4.	*Ibid.*	She put it . . .
iii, 2.	*Ibid.*	An' so we made a reel O
iii, 3.	*Ibid.*	. . . bony lass . . .
iii, 4.	*Ibid.*	. . . malt . . .
Chorus		Only first line given in Herd's MS.

MY AIN KIND DEARIE

TUNE: *The Lea Rig*

ᴏ◆ᴏ

From MMC. Basis of Burns's song "The Lea Rig" (HH III, 284). The first stanza (identical, except for the refrain "My ain kind deary O," and "I'll rowe thee" for "I'll lay thee") is quoted by Burns in the Interleaved SMM (JCD. *N* 17) as "the old words of this song . . . which were mostly composed by poor [Robert] Ferguson, in one of his merry humours."

ᴏ◆ᴏ

I'll lay thee o'er the lee-rig,
  Lovely Mary, deary, O;
I'll lay thee o'er the lee-rig,
  My lovely Mary, deary, O.
Altho' the night were ne'er so wet,
  An' I were ne'er so weary O;
I'd lay thee o'er the lee-rig,
  My lovely Mary, deary, O.

Look down ye gods from yonder sky,
  An' see how blest a man am I;
No envy my fond heart alarms,
  Encircled in my Mary's arms.
Lyin' across the lee-rig,
  Wi' lovely Mary, deary, O;
Lyin' across the lee-rig,
  Wi' my ain kind deary, O.

[131]

SHE ROSE AND LOOT ME IN

❧❖❧

From MMC. Origin of Burns's song "Tho' cruel fate should bid
us part" (HH iii, 12), often attributed to Francis Semple of
Beltrees. A version in TTM (Dublin 1729, 128) purified by
Ramsay who, says Burns in the Interleaved SMM, "I believe
it was . . . took it into his head to clear it of some seeming
indelicacies, and made it at once more chaste and more dull"
(JCD. *N* 20). "The original song . . . with the music," says
Dick (JCD. *N* 89), "is in Playford's *Choyce Ayres* 1685."

❧❖❧

The night her silent sable wore,
    An' gloomin' was the skies;
O' glitt'rin' stars appear'd no more
    Than those in Nelly's eyes:
When at her father's gate I knock'd,
    Where I had often been;
Shrouded only in her smock,
    She rose an' loot me in.

Fast lock'd within my fond embrace,
    She tremblin' stood asham'd;
Her glowin' lips an' heavin' breasts,
    At every touch enflam'd;
My eager passion I obey'd,
    Resolv'd the fort to win;
An' she, at last, gave her consent
    To yeild an' let me in.

O then! what bliss beyond compare,
    I knew no greater joy;
Enroll'd in heavenly happiness,
    So bless'd a man was I;

An' she, all ravish'd with delight,
　　Bad me aft come again,
An' kindly vow'd that ev'ry night
　　She'd rise an' let me in.

But ah! at last, she prov'd wi' bairn,
　　An' sat baith sad an' dull;
An' I wha was as much concern'd,
　　Look'd e'en just like a fool;
Her lovely eyes wi' tears ran o'er,
　　Repentin' her rash sin;
An' ay she curs'd the fatal hour
　　That e'er she loot me in.

But, who cou'd from such beauty go,
　　Or yet from Nelly part;
I lov'd her dear, an' couldna leave
　　The charmer of my heart,
We wedded and conceal'd our crime,
　　Then all was weel again,
An' now she blesses the happy night
　　She rose an' loot me in.

i, 3.　MMC misprints　"no more appear'd"
iii, 1.　MMC misprints　"bless"

THE COOPER O' DUNDEE

TUNE: *Bonny Dundee*

∽✧∽

From MMC. An old version of "Whare gat ye that happed meal-bannock?" (HH III, 2).

∽✧∽

Ye coopers and hoopers attend to my ditty,
  I sing o' a cooper who dwelt in Dundee;
This young man he was baith am'rous and witty,
  He pleas'd the fair maids wi' the blink o' his e'e.

He was nae a cooper, a common tub-hooper,
  The most o' his trade lay in pleasin' the fair;
He hoopt them, he coopt them, he bort them, he plugt
    them.
  An' a' sent for Sandie when out o' repair.

For a twelvemonth or sae this youth was respected,
  An' he was as bisie, as weel he could be;
But bis'ness increas'd so, that some were neglected,
  Which ruin'd trade in the town o' Dundee.

A baillie's fair daughter had wanted a coopin',
  An' Sandie was sent for, as oft time was he,
He yerkt her sae hard that she sprung an end-hoopin',
  Which banish'd poor Sandie frae bonny Dundee.

WILL YE NA, CAN YE NA, LET ME BE

TUNE: *I ha'e laid a herrin' in sa't*

⚬◈⚬

From MMC. First lines paraphrased in "Scroggam" (HH III, 192).

⚬◈⚬

There liv'd a wife in Whistle-cockpen,
　Will ye na, can ye na, let me be,
She brews gude yill for gentleman,
　And ay she waggit it wantonlie.

The night blew sair wi' wind and weet,
　Will ye na, can ye na, let me be,
She shaw'd the traveller ben to sleep,
　And ay she waggit it wantonlie.

She saw a sight below his sark,
　Will ye na, can ye na, let me be,
She wadna wanted it for a mark,
　And ay she waggit it wantonlie.

She saw a sight aboon his knee,
　Will ye na, can ye na, let me be,
She wadna wanted it for three,
　And ay she waggit it wantonlie.

O whare live ye, and what's your trade?
　Will ye na, can ye na, let me be,
I am a thresher gude, he said,
　And ay she waggit it wantonlie.

And that's my flail and workin' graith,
　Will ye na, can ye na, let me be,

And noble tools, quo' she, by my faith!
    And ay she waggit it wantonlie.

I wad gie a browst, the best I hae,
    Will ye na, can ye na, let me be,
For a gude darge o' graith like thae,
    And ay she waggit it wantonlie.

I wad sell the hair frae aff my tail,
    Will ye na, can ye na, let me be,
To buy our Andrew siccan a flail,
    And ay she waggit it wantonlie.

ELLIBANKS

◇

From MMC. Original of song of same name attributed to Burns
(*B.Chr.* II, 1893, 152). Burns, in his *Journal of the Border Tour*
(ed. DLF 1943) with Robert Ainslie, records:

> Monday [May 14, 1787]—Come to Inverleithing [Inner-
> leithen, to-day] a famous Spaw, & in the vicinity of the
> palace of Traquair, where having dined, and drank some
> Galloway-whey, I here remain till to-morrow—saw Elibanks
> and Elibraes so famous in baudy song today—on the other
> side of Tweed.

In November, 1791(?), Burns wrote to Ainslie from Dumfries
(DLF. *L* II, 99):

> . . . When I tell you even c——* has lost its power to please
> you will guess something of my hell within and all around
> me. I began "Elibanks and Elibraes," but the stanzas fell
> unenjoyed, and unfinished from my listless tongue.

The final stanza, says SD in a pencilled note in MMC, is
"Burns's addendum." The first two stanzas, he says, are
"printed in a Dublin Collection 1769." We have failed to trace
this work.

◇

Ellibanks and Ellibraes,
   My blessin's ay befa' them,
Tho' I wish I had brunt a' my claes,
   The first time e'er I saw them:
Your succar kisses were sac sweet,
   Deil d——n me gin I ken, man,
How ye gart me lay my legs aside,
   And lift my sark mysel, man.

---

* Scott Douglas's text in MMC, holograph addenda.

[187]

There's no a lass in a' the land,
    Can f—k sae weel as I can;
Louse down your breeks, lug out your wand,
    Hae ye nae mind to try, man:
For ye're the lad that wears the breeks,
    And I'm the lass that loes ye;
Deil rive my c—t to candle-wicks,
    Gif ever I refuse ye!!!

I'll clasp my arms about your neck,
    As souple as an eel, jo;
I'll cleek my houghs about your a—e,
    As I were gaun to speel, jo;
I'll cleek my houghs about your a—e,
    As I were gaun to speel, jo;
And if Jock thief he should slip out,
    I'll ding him wi' my heel, jo.

Green be the broom on Ellibraes,
    And yellow be the gowan!
My wame it fistles ay like flaes,
    As I come o'er the knowe, man:
There I lay glowran to the moon,
    Your mettle wadna daunton,
For hard your hurdies hotch'd aboon,
    While I below lay panting.

COMIN' THRO' THE RYE

⚬❖⚬

From MMC. Original of Burns's song of same name (HH III,
151). A pencilled note beside stanza iii reads: "Written on a
window of the Globe, Dumfries."

⚬❖⚬

O gin a body meet a body,
 Comin' throu the rye;
Gin a body f—k a body,
 Need a body cry.

  Comin' thro' the rye, my jo,
   An' comin' thro' the rye;
  She fand a staun o' staunin' graith,
   Comin' thro' the rye.

Gin a body meet a body,
 Comin' thro' the glen;
Gin a body f—k a body,
 Need the warld ken.

Gin a body meet a body,
 Comin' thro' the grain;
Gin a body f—k a body,
 C—t's a body's ain.

Gin a body meet a body,
 By a body's sel,
What na body f—s a body,
 Wad a body tell.

Mony a body meets a body,
 They dare na weel avow;
Mony a body f—s a body,
 Ye wadna think it true.

AS I CAM O'ER THE CAIRNEY MOUNT

TUNE: *Highland Laddie*

ᴏ❖ᴏ

From MMC. Original of Burns's song of same name (HH III, 171). A purified version by Allan Ramsay in TTM 1724 (169). Burns wrote to Thomson (September, 1793): "The old Highland Laddie . . . is sometimes called Ginglan Johnie; it being the air of an old humorous bawdy song of that name— You will find it in the Museum, vol; 4th P. 342" (DLF, *L* II, 201). Burns's note in the Interleaved SMM runs: "The first and indeed the most beautiful set of this tune was formerly, and in some places is still known by the name of 'As I cam o'er the Cairney Mount,' which is the first line of an excellent but somewhat licentious song still sung to the tune" (JCD. *N* 8).

ᴏ❖ᴏ

As I cam o'er the Cairney mount,
   And down amang the blooming heather,
The Highland laddie drew his durk
   And sheath'd it in my wanton leather.

     O my bonnie, bonnie Highland lad,
     My handsome, charming Highland laddie;
     When I am sick and like to die,
     He'll row me in his Highland plaiddie.

With me he play'd his warlike pranks,
   And on me boldly did adventure,
He did attack me on both flanks,
   And pushed me fiercely in the centre.

A furious battle then began,
   Wi' equal courage and desire,
Altho' he struck me three to one,
   I stood my ground and receiv'd his fire.

But our ammunition being spent,
    And we quite out o' breath an' sweating,
We did agree with ae consent,
    To fight it out at the next meeting.

JOHN ANDERSON, MY JO

❧❧❧

From MMC. Basis for Burns's famous song of same name (HH
III, 63). The version in M'N agrees verbatim with MM27 where
it is claimed to have been taken from a songbook of 1782.
Other versions in *Philomel* (London, 1744) and *The Masque*
(London, 1768). Square brackets indicate torn page in MMC.

❧❧❧

John Anderson, my jo, John,
 I wonder what ye mean,
To lie sae lang i' the mornin',
 And sit sae late at e'en?
Ye'll bleer a' your een, John,
 And why do ye so?
Come sooner to your bed at een,
 John Anderson, my jo.

John Anderson, my jo, John,
 When first that ye began,
Ye had as good a tail-tree,
 As ony ither man;
But now its waxen wan, John,
 And wrinkles to and fro;
[I've t] wa gae-ups for ae gae-down,
 [John] Anderson, my jo.

[I'm ba]ckit like a salmon,
 [I'm] breastit like a swan;
My wame it is a down-cod,
 My middle ye may span:
Frae my tap-knot to my tae, John,
 I'm like the new-fa'n snow;
And it's a' for your convenience,
 John Anderson, my jo.

O it is a fine thing
    To keep out o'er the dyke;
But its a meikle finer thing,
    To see your hurdies fyke;
To see your hurdies fyke, John,
    And hit the rising blow;
It's then I like your chanter-pipe,
    John Anderson, my jo.

When ye come on before, John,
    See that ye do your best;
When ye begin to haud me,
    See that ye grip me fast;
See that ye grip me fast, John,
    Until that I cry "Oh!"
Your back shall crack or I do that,
    John Anderson, my jo.

John Anderson, my jo, John,
    Ye're welcome when ye please;
It's either in the warm bed
    Or else aboon the claes:
Or ye shall hae the horns, John,
    Upon your head to grow;
An' that's the cuckold's mallison,
    John Anderson, my jo.

DUNCAN DAVIDSON

❧❖❧

From MMC. Basis of Burns's song of same name (HH III, 19).

❧❖❧

There was a lass, they ca'd her Meg,
   An' she gaed o'er the muir to spin;
She fee'd a lad to lift her leg,
   They ca'd him Duncan Davidson.
                    Fal, lal, &c.

Meg had a muff and it was rough,
   Twas black without and red within,
An' Duncan, case he got the cauld,
   He stole his highland p—e in.
                    Fal, lal, &c.

Meg had a muff, and it was rough,
   And Duncan strak tway handfu' in;
She clasp'd her heels about his waist,
   "I thank you Duncan! Yerk it in!!!"
                    Fal, lal, &c.

Duncan made her hurdies dreep,
   In Highland wrath, then Meg did say;
O gang he east, or gang he west,
   His ba's will no be dry today.

THE PLOUGHMAN

⌁

From MMC. Original of Burns's song of same name (HH III,
24). M'Naught's note reads: "A purified version will be found
in Herd [1769, 317]. Scott Douglas prints another version in
his Kilmarnock edition (I, 222). The parable of the 'three
owsen,' begun in the fourth stanza, is found in the 'Auld White
Nag,' a licentious ditty current in Ayrshire to this day, the
'owsen' being changed into 'pownies.' It also is evidently old.

" 'Then he drew out his horses which were in number three,
Three likelier pownies for to draw, their like ye ne'er did see
There was twa dun pownies on ahin', auld Whitey on afore,
The muzzle-pin for a' the yirth was in the highest bore.

" 'Before he gat the hause-rig turned his horse began to sweat,
And to maintain an open fur, he spurred wi' baith his feet'
&c."

⌁

The ploughman he's a bonnie lad,
    His mind is ever true, jo;
His garters knit below the knee,
    His bonnet it is blue, jo.

Sing up wi't a', the ploughman lad,
And hey the merry ploughman;
O' a' the trades that I do ken,
Commend me to the ploughman.

As wakin' forth upon a day,
    I met a jolly ploughman,
I tald him I had lands to plough,
    If he wad prove true, man.

He says, my dear, tak ye nae fear,
    I'll fit you till a hair jo;

I'll cleave it up, and hit it down,
   And water-furrow't fair, jo.

I hae three ousen in my plough,
   Three better ne'er plough'd ground, jo.
The foremost ox is lang and sma',
   The twa are plump and round, jo.

Then he wi' speed did yoke his plough,
   Which by a gaud was driven, jo!
But when he wan between the stilts,
   I thought I was in heaven, jo!

But the foremost ox fell in the fur,
   The tither twa did founder;
The ploughman lad he breathless grew,
   In faith it was nae wonder.

But a sykie risk, below the hill,
   The plough she took a stane, jo,
Which gart the fire flee frae the sock,
   The ploughman gied a grane, jo.

I hae plough'd east, I hae plough'd west,
   In weather foul and fair, jo;
But the sairest ploughing e'er I plough'd,
   Was ploughing amang hair, jo.

    Sing up wi't a', and in wi't a',
    And hey my merry ploughman;
    O' a' the trades, and crafts I ken,
    Commend me to the ploughman.

ii, 1.   wakin', *i.e.* walkin'

ANDREW AN' HIS CUTTIE GUN

From MMC. Original of Burns's song "Blythe was she" (HH
III, 29). Described by him in a letter to George Thomson
(November 19, 1794) as "the work of a Master" (DFL, *L* II,
276). "Burns's song was modelled on the brilliant vernacular
bacchanalian 'Andro and his cutty gun,' which is the original
or a parody of verses in *The Merry Muses*" (JCD. *N* 96). The
drinking-song version appeared in TTM 1740 (423) and is
indeed brilliant. It begins:

> Blyth blyth, blyth was she,
> Blyth was she butt and ben;
> And weel she loo'd a Hawick gill
> And leuch to see a tappit hen.

Hawick gills were renowned for their heroic proportions.

> When a' the lave gaed to their bed,
> And I sat up to clean the shoon,
> O wha think ye cam jumpin' ben,
> But Andrew and his cuttie gun.

> Blythe, blythe, blythe was she,
> Blythe was she but and ben,
> An' weel she lo'ed it in her neive,
> But better when it slippit in.

> Or e'er I wist he laid me back,
> And up my gamon to my chin,
> And ne'er a word to me he spak,
> But liltit out his cutty gun.

> The bawsent bitch she left the whalps,
> And hunted round us at the fun,
> As Andrew fodgel'd wi his a—e,
> And fir'd at me the cuttie gun.

[147]

O some delights in cuttie stoup,
   And some delights in cuttie-mun,
But my delight's an a—elins coup,
   Wi' Andrew an' his cuttie gun.

O CAN YE LABOUR LEE, YOUNG MAN?

TUNE: *Sir Arch. Grant's Strathspey*

✧

From MMC. Original of Burns's song of same name (HH III, 138). Attributed to Burns by GL.

✧

I fee'd a man at Martinmas,
　　Wi arle pennies three;
But a' the fau't I had to him,
　　He coudna labour lee.

　　　O can ye labour lee, young man,
　　　　O can ye labour lee;
　　　Gae back the road ye cam agin,
　　　　Ye shall never scorn me.

A stibble rig is easy plough'd,
　　An' fallow land is free;
But what a silly coof is he,
　　That canna labour lee.

The spretty bush, an' benty knowe,
　　The ploughman points his sock in,
He sheds the roughness, lays it by,
　　An' bauldly ploughs his yokin'.

IV

◦◆◦

COLLECTED
BY BURNS

Notes in this section are by
SYDNEY GOODSIR SMITH
unless otherwise initialled

THE REELS O' BOGIE

TUNE: *Cauld Kail in Aberdeen*

❖

From MM27. Not in MMC. Purified version in SMM (II, 170)
with words by the Duke of Gordon. This below is a very
corrupt and anglicized text: for an idea of what the original
was like, compare stanza iii with the old version known to
Burns (in Section I B, "There Cam a Soger"). Another version
in DH 1769 (314).

❖

You lads and lasses all that dwell
   In the town of Strathbogie,
Whene'er you meet a pretty lass,
   Be sure you tip her cogie.
The lads and lasses toy and kiss,
   The lads ne'er think it is amiss
To bang the holes whereout they piss,
   And that's the reels o' Bogie.

There's Kent, and Keen, and Aberdeen,
   And the town of Strathbogie,
Where every lad may have his lass,
   Now that I've got my cogie.
They spread wide their snow-white thighs
   And roll about their wanton eyes,
And when they see your pintle rise
   They'll dance the reels o' Bogie.

A trooper going o'er the lea,
   He swore that he would steer me,
And long before the break of day,
   He giggled, goggled near me.
He put a stiff thing in my hand,
   I could not bear the banging o't

But long before he went away
  I suppled both the ends o't.

His pintle was of largest size,
  Indeed it was a banger,
He sought a prize between my thighs
  Till it became a hanger.
Had you but seen the wee bit skin
  He had to put his pintle in,
You'd sworn it was a chitterling
  Dancing the reels o' Bogie.

He turned about to fire again
  And give me t'other sally,
And as he fired I ne'er retired
  But received him in my alley.
His pebbles they went thump, thump,
  Against my little wanton rump,
But soon I left him but the stump
  To dance the reels o' Bogie.

Said I, young man, more you can't do,
  I think I've granted your desire,
By bobbing on my wanton clue,
  You see your pintle's all on fire.
When on my back I work like steel
  And bar the door with my left heel,
The more you f— the less I feel,
  And that's the reels o' Bogie.

iv, 1. MM27 (another edn.) . . . largcish size.
v, 7. *Ibid.* . . . with the stump.

JOCKEY WAS A BONNY LAD

TUNE: *John Roy Stewart's Strathspey*

◇◇◇

From MMC. Another version in DH 1791 (ii, 325). The changes
are all improvements poetically and were almost certainly
made by Burns when transcribing the song.

◇◇◇

My jockey is a bonny lad,
A dainty lad, a merry lad,
A neat sweet pretty little lad,
   An' just the lad for me.
For when we o'er the meadows stray,
He's ay sae lively ay sae gay,
An' aft right canty does he say,
   There's nane he loes like me.

     An' he's ay huggin' ay dawtin',
     Ay clappin', ay pressin',
     Ay squeezin', ay kissin',
       An' winna let me be.

I met my lad the ither day,
Friskin' thro' a field o' hay,
Says he, dear Jenny, will ye stay,
   An' crack a while wi' me.
Na, Jockey lad, I darena stay,
My mither she'd miss me away;
Syne she'll flyte an' scauld a' day,
   An' play the diel wi' me.

   But Jockey still continued, &c.

Hoot! Jockey, see my hair is down,
An' look you've torn a' my gown,

[155]

An' how will I gae thro' the town,
  Dear laddie tell to me.
He never minded what I said,
But wi' my neck an' bosom play'd;
Tho' I intreated, begg'd an' pray'd
  Him no to touzle me.

    But Jockey still continued
    Huggin', dawtin', clappin', squeezin',
    An' ay kissin', kissin', kissin',
      Till down cam we.

As breathless an' fatigued I lay,
In his arms among the hay,
My blood fast thro' my veins did play
  As he lay huggin' me;
I thought my breath wou'd never last,
For Jockey danc'd sae devilish fast;
But what cam o'er, I trow, at last,
  There diel ane kens but me.

    But soon he weari'd o' his dance,
    O' a' his jumpin' an' his prance,
    An' confess'd without romance,
      He was fain to let me be.

i, 5. MMC misprints "he" for "we"
ii, 2. MMC misprints "a hay" for "o' hay"

BLYTH WILL AN' BESSIE'S WEDDING

TUNE: *Roy's Wife*

⋄◈⋄

From MMC. Stanza iv, says Scott Douglas in a pencilled note in
MMC, is "Burns's addendum."

⋄◈⋄

There was a weddin' o'er in Fife,
　　An' mony ane frae Lothian at it;
Jean Vernor there maist lost hir life,
　　For love o' Jamie Howden at it.

　　　Blyth Will an' Bessie's weddin',
　　　Blyth Will an' Bessie's weddin',
　　　Had I been Will, Bess had been mine,
　　　An' Bess an' I had made the weddin'.

Right sair she grat, an' wet her cheeks,
　　An' naithing pleas'd that we cou'd gie her;
She tint her heart in Jeamie's breeks,
　　It cam nae back to Lothian wi' her.

[Tam]mie Tamson too was there,
　　Maggie Birnie was his dearie,
He pat it in amang the hair,
　　An' puddled there till he was weary.

When e'enin' cam the town was thrang,
　　An' beds were no to get for siller;
When e'er they fand a want o' room,
　　They lay in pairs like bread an' butter.

Twa an' twa they made the bed,
　　An' twa an' twa they lay the gither;
When they had na room enough,
　　Ilk ane lap on aboon the tither.

[157]

THE LASS O' LIVISTON

◦✦◦

From MMC. There is a purified version by Allan Ramsay in
TTM 1724 (99). Burns's note in the Interleaved Copy of SMM
reads: ". . . The original set of verses to this tune is still
extant, and have a very great deal of poetic merit, but are not
quite ladies' reading" (JCD. *N* 6). Scott Douglas in a pencilled
note in MMC says. "Old song revised by Burns."

◦✦◦

The bonny lass o' Liviston,
  Her name ye ken, her name ye ken;
And ay the welcomer ye'll be,
  The farther ben, the farther ben,
And she has it written in her contract
  To lie her lane, to lie her lane,
And I hae written in my contract
  To claw her wame, to claw her wame.

The bonny lass o' Liviston,
  She's berry brown, she's berry brown;
An' ye winna true her lovely locks,
  Gae farther down, gae farther down.
She has a black and a rolling eye,
  And a dimplit chin, and a dimplit chin;
And no to prie her rosy lips,
  Wad be a sin, wad be a sin.

The bonny lass o' Liviston,
  Cam in to me, cam in to me;
I wat wi' baith ends o' the busk,
  I made me free, I made me free.

I laid her feet to my bed-stock,
   Her head to the wa', her head to the wa';
And I gied her her wee coat in her teeth,
   Her sark an' a', her sark an' a'.

iii, 7.　MMC misprints　"wi'" for "wee"

HE'S HOY'D ME OUT O' LAUDERDALE

ᴏ❖ᴏ

From MMC. Line 5, stanza iii, is incorporated in Burns's song "The Deuk's Dang o'er my Daddie, O!" (HH iii, 139). Scott Douglas in a pencilled note in MMC says, "Old song revised by Burns."

ᴏ❖ᴏ

There liv'd a lady in Lauderdale,
    She lo'ed a fiddler fine;
She lo'ed him in her chamber,
    She held him in her mind;
She made his bed at her bed-stock,
    She said he was her brither;
But she's hoy'd him out o' Lauderdale,
    His fiddle and a' thegither.

First when I cam to Lauderdale,
    I had a fiddle gude,
My sounding-pin stood like the aik
    That grows in Lauder-wood;
But now my sounding-pin's gaen down,
    And tint the foot forever;
She's hoy'd me out o' Lauderdale,
    My fiddle and a' thegither.

First when I came to Lauderdale,
    Your Ladyship can declare,
I play'd a bow, a noble bow,
    As e'er was strung wi' hair;
But dow'na do's come o'er me now,
    And your Ladyship winna consider;
She's hoy'd me out o' Lauderdale,
    My fiddle and a' thegither.

ERROCK BRAE

TUNE: *Sir Alex. Don's Strathspey*

❧❦❧

From MMC, where Scott Douglas comments, "Old song
revised by Burns."

❧❦❧

O Errock stane, may never maid,
   A maiden by thee gae,
Nor e'er a stane o' stanin' graith,
   Gae stanin' o'er the brae.

      And tillin' Errock brae, young man,
         An' tillin' Errock brae,
         An open fur an' stanin' graith,
         Maun till the Errock brae.

As I sat by the Errock stane,
   Surveying far and near,
Up cam a Cameronian,
   Wi' a' his preaching gear.

He flang the Bible o'er the brae,
   Amang the rashy gerse;
But the solemn league and covenant
   He laid below my a—e.

But on the edge of Errock brae,
   He gae me sic a sten,
That o'er, and o'er, and o'er we row'd,
   Till we cam to the glen.

Yet still his p——e held the grip,
   And still his b——s hang;

That a Synod cou'd na tell the a—e
    To whom they did belang.

A Prelate he loups on before,
    A Catholic behin',
But gie me a Cameronian,
    He'll m—w a body blin'.

YE HAE LIEN WRANG, LASSIE

TUNE: *Up and waur them a', Willie*

ᚬ❖ᚬ

From MMC. Attributed to Burns by GL.

ᚬ❖ᚬ

Your rosy cheeks are turn'd sae wan,
  Ye're greener than the grass, lassie,
Your coatie's shorter by a span,
  Yet deil an inch the less, lassie.

  Ye hae lien wrang, lassie,
    Ye've lien a' wrang,
  Ye've lien in some unco bed,
    And wi' some unco man.

Ye've loot the pounie o'er the dyke,
  And he's been in the corn, lassie;
For ay the brose ye sup at e'en,
  Ye bock them or the morn, lassie.

Fu' lightly lap ye o'er the knowe,
  And thro' the wood ye sang, lassie;
But herryin' o' the foggie byke,
  I fear ye've got a stang, lassie.

COMIN' O'ER THE HILLS O' COUPAR

TUNE: *Ruffian's Rant*

◇❖◇

From MMC, where stanzas iv–vi are incorporated in "Blyth
Will and Bessie's Wedding." We follow M'Naught in trans-
planting them. As he says, "they seem to be . . . from
another ditty much resembling 'Comin' o'er the Hills o'
Coupar.' " Attributed to Burns by GL.

◇❖◇

Donald Brodie met a lass,
   Comin' o'er the hills o' Coupar,
Donald wi' his Highland hand
   Graipit a' the bits about her.

      Comin' o'er the hills o' Coupar,
      Comin' o'er the hills o' Coupar,
      Donald in a sudden wrath
      He ran his Highland durk into her.

Weel I wat she was a quine,
   Wad made a body's mouth to water;
Our Mess John, wi's auld grey pow,
   His haly lips wad licket at her.

Up she started in a fright,
   Thro' the braes what she could bicker:
Let her gang, quo' Donald, now
   For in him's nerse * my shot is sicker.

*   *   *

---

* *him's nerse* = her arse; a joke at expense of Highlanders' traditional
muddling of genders.

[164]

Kate Mackie cam frae Parlon craigs,
　The road was foul twixt that an' Couper;
She shaw'd a pair o' handsome legs,
　When Highland Donald he o'ertook her.

　　Comin' o'er the moor o' Couper,
　　Comin' o'er the moor o' Couper,
　　Donald fell in love wi' her
　　An' row'd his Highland plaid about her.

They took them to the Logan steps
　An' set them down to rest thegither,
Donald laid her on her back
　An' fir'd a Highland pistol at her.

Lochleven Castle heard the rair,
　An' Falkland-house the echo sounded;
Highland Donald gae a stare,
　The lassie sigh'd, but was nae wounded.

ii, 3.　MMC misprints "we's"
iii, 2.　what . . . bicker, i.e. as fast as she could.

HOW CAN I KEEP MY MAIDENHEAD?

TUNE: *The Birks o' Abergeldie*

ༀ❖ༀ

From MMC. Another version, almost certainly by Burns, in the
Cunningham MS is printed in *The Horn Book* (GL, 137).

ༀ❖ༀ

How can I keep my maidenhead,
   My maidenhead, my maidenhead;
How can I keep my maidenhead,
   Among sae mony men, O.

The Captain bad a guinea for't,
   A guinea for't, a guinea for't;
The Captain bad a guinea for't,
   The Colonel he bad ten, O.

But I'll do as my minnie did,
   My minnie did, my minnie did;
But I'll do as my minnie did,
   For siller I'll hae nane, O.

I'll gie it to a bonie lad,
   A bonie lad, a bonie lad;
I'll gie it to a bonie lad,
   For just as gude again, O.

An auld moulie maidenhead,
   A maidenhead, a maidenhead;
An auld moulie maidenhead,
   The weary wark I ken, O.

The stretchin' o't, the strivin' o't,
   The borin' o't, the rivin' o't,
And ay the double drivin' o't,
   The farther ye gang ben, O.

[166]

WAD YE DO THAT?

TUNE: *John Anderson, my jo*

◇◆◇

From MMC. Attributed to Burns by GL.

◇◆◇

Gudewife, when your gudeman's frae hame,
 Might I but be sae bauld,
As come to your bed-chamber,
 When winter nights are cauld;
As come to your bed-chamber,
 When nights are cauld and wat,
And lie in your gudeman's stead,
 Wad ye do that?

Young man, an ye should be so kind,
 When our gudeman's frae hame,
As come to my bed-chamber,
 Where I am laid my lane;
And lie in our gudeman's stead,
 I will tell you what,
He f—s me five times ilka night,
 Wad ye do that?

THERE CAM A CADGER

TUNE: *Clout the Cauldron*

❧❧❧

From MMC. Attributed to Burns by GL.

❧❧❧

There cam a cadger out o' Fife,
　I watna how they ca'd him;
He play'd a trick to our gudewife,
　When fient a body bad him.

　　　　　　　Fal, lal, &c.

He took a lang thing stout and strang,
　An' strack it in her gyvel;
An' ay she swore she fand the thing
　Gae borin' by her nyvel.

　　　　　　　Fal, lal, &c.

JENNY MACRAW

TUNE: *The bonny moor-hen*

☞❖☜

From MMC. Attributed to Burns in Cunningham MS (GL, 135).

☞❖☜

Jenny Macraw was a bird o' the game,
An' mony a shot had been lows'd at her wame;
Be't a lang bearing arrow, or the sharp-rattlin' hail,
Still, whirr! she flew off wi' the shot in her tail.

Jenny Macraw to the mountains she's gaen,
Their leagues and their covenants a' she has taen;
My head now, and heart now, quo' she, are at rest,
An' for my poor c—t, let the deil do his best.

Jenny Macraw on a midsummer morn,
She cut off her c—t and she hang't on a thorn;
There she loot it hing for a year and a day,
But, oh! how look'd her a—e when her c—twas away.

OUR GUDEWIFE'S SAE MODEST

TUNE: *John Anderson, my jo*

ᴐ✦ᴐ

From MMC.

ᴐ✦ᴐ

Our gudewife's sae modest,
  When she is set at meat,
A laverock's leg, or a tittling's wing,
  Is mair than she can eat;
But, when she's in her bed at e'en,
  Between me and the wa';
She is a glutton deevil,
  She swallows c—s an a'.

SUPPER IS NA READY

TUNE: *Clout the Cauldron*

o❖o

From MMC.

o❖o

Roseberry to his lady says,
  "My hinnie and my succour,
"O shall we do the thing you ken,
  "Or shall we take our supper?"
      Fal, lal, &c.

Wi' modest face, sae fu' o' grace,
  Replied the bonny lady;
"My noble lord do as you please,
  "But supper is na ready."
      Fal, lal, &c.

Un frais mary dit à sa Damoiselle;
Souperons nous, ou ferons le deduit?
Faisons lequel qu'il vous plaira, dit-elle,
Mais le souper n'est pas encore cuit.

  (From *Jeux et Desduits*, ed. A. t'Serstevens, Paris 1946. "Anon. XVIe siècle".

Transmitted to me by G. Legman. [SGS]

[**171**]

YON, YON, YON, LASSIE

TUNE: *Ruffian's Rant*

ᴑ◈ᴑ

From MMC, where Scott Douglas gives the tune as "Cameron's got his wife again."

ᴑ◈ᴑ

I never saw a silken gown,
　　But I wad kiss the sleeve o't;
I never saw a maidenhead
　　That I wad spier the leave o't.

　　O, yon, yon, yon, lassie,
　　　　Yon, yon, yon;
　　I never met a bonie lass
　　　　But what wad play at yon.

Tell nae me, o' Meg my wife,
　　That crowdie has na savour;
But gie to me a bonie lass
　　An' let me steal the favour.

Gie me her I kis't yestreen,
　　I vow but she was handsome,
For ilka birss upon her c—t,
　　Was worth a royal ransom.

　　An' yon, yon, yon, lassie,
　　　　Yon, yon, yon,
　　I never saw a bonie lass
　　　　But what wad do yon.

THE YELLOW, YELLOW YORLIN'

TUNE: *Bonnie beds of roses*

ᴏ◆ᴏ

From MMC., where Scott Douglas gives the tune as "The Collier Laddie."

ᴏ◆ᴏ

It fell on a day, in the flow'ry month o' May,
   All on a merry merry mornin',
I met a pretty maid, an' unto her I said,
   I wad fain fin' your yellow yellow yorlin'.

O no, young man, says she, you're a stranger to me,
   An' I am anither man's darlin',
Wha has baith sheep an' cows, that's feedin' in the
     hows,
   An' a cock for my yellow yellow yorlin'.

But, if I lay you down upon the dewy ground,
   You wad nae be the waur ae farthing;
An' that happy, happy man, he never wou'd ken
   That I play'd wi' your yellow yellow yorlin'.

O fie, young man, says she, I pray you let me be,
   I wad na for five pound sterling;
My mither wad gae mad, an' sae wad my dad,
   If you play'd wi' my yellow yellow yorlin'.

But I took her by the waist, an' laid her down in haste,
   For a' her squakin' and squalin';
The lassie soon grew tame, an' bade me come again
   For to play wi' her yellow yellow yorlin'.

SHE GRIPET AT THE GIRTEST O'T

TUNE: *East Nook of Fife*

o◆o

From MMC.

o◆o

Our bride flate, and our bride flang,
But lang before the laverock sang,
She pay't him twice for every bang,
   And gripet at the girtest o't.

Our bride turn'd her to the wa',
But lang before the cock did craw,
She took him by the b——ks and a',
   And gripet at the girtest o't.

YE'SE GET A HOLE TO HIDE IT IN

TUNE: *Waukin' o' the Fauld*

༊❖༊

From MMC.

ᴏ❖ᴏ

O will ye speak at our town,
    As ye come frae the fair?
And ye'se get a hole to hide it in,
    Ye'se get a hole to hide it in;
Will ye speak at our town
    As ye come frae the fair,
Ye'se get a hole to hide it in,
    Will haud it a' and mair.

O haud awa your hand, Sir,
    Ye gar me ay think shame;
An' ye'se get a hole to hide it in;
    Ye'se get a hole to hide it in;
O haud awa your hand, Sir,
    Ye gar me ay think shame;
An' ye'se get a hole to hide it in,
    An' think yoursel at hame.

O will ye let abee, Sir;
    Toots! now, ye've rivt my sark,
An' ye'se get a hole to hide it in,
    Ye'se get a hole to hide it in;
O will ye let abee, Sir;
    Toots! now, ye've reft my sark;
An' ye'se get a hole to hide it in,
    Whare ye may work your wark.

O haud awa your hand, Sir,
　Ye're like to pit me daft;
And ye'se get a hole to hide it in,
　Ye'se get a hole to hide it in;
O had awa your hand, Sir,
　Ye're like to put me daft;
An' ye'se get a hole to hide it in,
　To keep it warm and saft.

O had it in your hand, Sir,
　Till I get up my claes,
An' ye'se get a hole to hide it in,
　Ye'se get a hole to hide it in;
O had it in your hand, Sir,
　Till I get up my claes;
An' ye'se get a hole to hide it in,
　To keep it frae the flaes.

i, 2.　MMC misprints "As ye came . . ."

DUNCAN MACLEERIE

TUNE: *Jocky Macgill*

ᐤ◈ᐤ

From MMC.

ᐤ◈ᐤ

Duncan Macleerie and Janet his wife,
They gaed to Kilmarnock to buy a new knife;
But instead of a knife they coft but a bleerie;
We're very weel saird. quo' Duncan Macleerie.

Duncan Macleerie has got a new fiddle,
It's a' strung wi' hair, and a hole in the middle;
An' ay when he plays on't, his wife looks sae cheary,
Very weel done, Duncan, quo' Janet Macleerie.

Duncan he play'd 'till his bow it grew greasy;
Janet grew fretfu', and unco uneasy.
Hoot, quo' she, Duncan, ye're unco soon weary;
Play us a pibroch, quo' Janet Macleerie.

Duncan Macleerie play'd on the harp,
An' Janet Macleerie danc'd in her sark;
Her sark it was short, her c—t it was hairy,
Very weel danc'd, Janet, quo' Duncan Macleerie.

iii, 4. The time for an average four-part march is two minutes; a pibroch 12 minutes. [JB]

THEY TOOK ME TO THE HALY BAND

TUNE: *Clout the Cauldron*

ᴏ◈ᴏ

From MMC.

ᴏ◈ᴏ

They took me to the haly band,
  For playing bye my wife, Sir;
And lang and sair they lectur'd me,
  For hadin' sic a life, Sir.

I answer'd in na mony words,
  "What deel needs a' this clatter;
"As lang as she cou'd keep the grip
  "I aye was m——g at her."

i, 2.   MMC misprints "me."

[178]

THE MODIEWARK

TUNE: *O for ane an' twenty, Tam*

ᴏ❖ᴏ

From MMC.

ᴏ❖ᴏ

The modiewark has done me ill,
And below my apron has biggit a hill;
I maun consult some learned clark
About this wanton modiewark.

An' O the wanton modiewark,
The weary wanton modiewark;
I maun consult some learned clark
About this wanton modiewark.

O first it gat between my taes,
Out o'er my garter niest it gaes;
At length it crap below my sark,
The weary wanton modiewark.

This modiewark, tho' it be blin';
If ance its nose you lat it in,
Then to the hilts, within a crack
It's out o' sight, the modiewark.

When Marjorie was made a bride,
An' Willy lay down by her side,
Syne nocht was hard, when a' was dark,
But kicking at the modiewark.

KEN YE NA OUR LASS, BESS?

TUNE: *Auld Sir Symon*

❖

From MMC. Attributed to Burns in Cunningham MS (GL, 186).

❖

O ken ye na our lass, Bess?
An' ken ye na our lass, Bess?
Between her lily white thies
She's biggit a magpie's nest.

An' ken ye na our lad, Tam?
An' ken ye na our lad, Tam?
He's on o' a three-fitted stool,
An' up to the nest he clamb.

An' what did he there, think ye?
An' what did he there, think ye?
He brak a' the eggs o' the nest,
An' the white's ran down her thie.

WHA THE DEIL CAN HINDER THE WIND TO BLAW?

TUNE: *Wat ye wha I met yestreen?*

❍❖❍

From MMC.

❍❖❍

It fell about the blythe new-year,
　When days are short and nights are lang,
Ae bonie night, the starns were clear,
　An' frost beneath my fit-stead rang;
I heard a carlin cry, "relief!"
　Atweesh her trams a birkie lay;
But he wan a quarter in her beef,
　For a' the jirts the carlin gae.

She heav'd to; and he strak frae,
　As he wad nail'd the carlin thro';
An' ilka f—t the carlin gae,
　It wad hae fill'd a pockie fou;
Temper your tail, the young man cried,
　Temper your tail by Venus' law!
Double your dunts, the dame replied,
　Wha the deil can hinder the wind to blaw?

Stanza ii is a variant of stanzas 2 and 3 of "Cumnock Psalms" (Section 1 B).

WE'RE A' GAUN SOUTHIE, O

TUNE: *The Merry Lads of Ayr*

❀

From MMC.

❀

Callum cam to Campbell's court,
  An' saw ye e'er the make o't;
Pay'd twenty shillings for a thing,
  An' never got a straik o't.

    We're a' gaun southie, O.
    We're a' gaun there;
    An' we're a' gaun to Mauchlin fair,
    To sell our pickle hair.

Pay'd twenty shillings for a quine,
  Her name was Kirsty Lauchlan;
But Callum took her by the c—t,
  Before the laird o' Mauchline.

Callum cam to Kirsty's door,
  Says, Kirsty are ye sleepin'?
No sae soun as ye wad trow,
  Ye'se get the thing ye're seekin'.

Callum had a peck o' meal,
  Says, Kirsty, will ye draik it?
She whippet off her wee white-coat,
  An' birket at it nakit.

Bonie lassie, braw lassie,
  Will ye hae a soger?
Then she took up her duddie sark,
  An' he shot in his Roger.

Kind kimmer Kirsty,
   I loe wi' a' my heart, O,
An' when there's ony p——s gaun,
   She'll ay get a part, O.

iv, 3.   MMC misprints   "of"

CUDDIE THE COOPER

TUNE: *Bonny Dundee*

ᴏ❖ᴏ

From MMC.

ᴏ❖ᴏ

There was a cooper they ca'd him Cuddy,
  He was the best cooper that ever I saw;
He came to girth our landlady's tubbie,
  He bang'd her buttocks again the wa'.

Cooper quo' she, hae ye ony mony?
  The deevil a penny, quo' Cuddy, at a'!
She took out her purse, an' she gied him a guinea,
  For banging her buttocks again the wa'.

NAE HAIR ON'T

TUNE: *Gillicrankie*

⚬✦⚬

From MMC, where Scott Douglas comments, "This is in the Dublin Collection, 1769."

⚬✦⚬

Yestreen I wed a lady fair,
    And ye wad believe me,
On her c—t there grows nae hair,
    That's the thing that grieves me.

It vexed me sair, it plagu'd me sair,
    It put me in a passion,
To think that I had wad a wife,
    Whase c—t was out o' fashion.

THERE'S HAIR ON'T

TUNE: *Push about the jorum*

ᴏ◈ᴏ

From MMC.

ᴏ◈ᴏ

O, ere yestreen I stented graith,
    An' labor'd lang an' sair on't;
But fient a work, na work wad it,
    There's sic a crap o' hair on't.

    There's hair on't, there's hair on't,
    There's thretty thrave an' mair on't;
    But gin I live to anither year,
    I'll tether my grey naigs on't.

An' up the glen there rase a knowe,
    Below the knowe a lair on't,
I maist had perish'd, fit an' horse,
    I could na see for hair on't.

But I'll plant a stake into the flowe,
    That ploughmen may tak care on't;
An' lay twa steppin'-stanes below,
    An' syne I'll cowe the hair on't.

THE LASSIE GATH'RING NITS

TUNE: *O the broom*

❧❖❧

From MMC.

❧❖❧

There was a lass, and a bonie lass,
    A gath'ring nits did gang;
She pu'd them heigh, she pu'd them laigh,
    She pu'd them whare they hang.

Till tir'd at length, she laid her down,
    An' sleept the wood amang;
Whan by there cam three lusty lads,
    Three lusty lads an' strang.

The first did kiss her rosy lips,
    He thought it was nae wrang;
The second lous'd her bodice fair,
    Fac'd up wi' London whang.

An' what the third did to the lass,
    I's no put in this sang;
But the lassie wauken'd in a fright,
    An' says, I hae sleept lang.

THE LINKIN' LADDIE

TUNE: *Push about the jorum*

ᴏ❖ᴏ

From MMC.

ᴏ❖ᴏ

Waes me that e'er I made your bed!
   Waes me that e'er I saw ye!
For now I've lost my maidenhead,
   An' I ken na how they ca' ye.

My name's weel kend in my ain countrie,
   They ca' me the linkin' laddie;
An' ye had na been as willing as I,
   Shame fa' them wad e'er hae bade ye.

JOHNIE SCOTT

TUNE: *O the broom*

o◆o

From MMC.

o◆o

Whare will we get a coat to Johnie Scott,
  Amang us maidens a'?
Whare will we get a coat to Johnie Scott,
  To mak the laddie braw:

There's your c—t-hair, and there's my c—t hair,
  An' we'll twine it wondrous sma';
An' if waft be scarce, we'll cowe our a—e,
  To mak him kilt an' a'.

MADGIE CAM TO MY BED-STOCK

TUNE: *Clout the Cauldron*

❍◈❍

From MMC.

❍◈❍

Madgie cam to my bed-stock,
  To see gif I was waukin;
I pat my han' atweesh her feet,
  An' fand her wee bit maukin.
    Fal, lal, &c.

C—t it was the sowen-pat,
  An' p——e was the ladle;
B—ks were the serving-men
  That waited at the table.
    Fal, lal, &c.

O GIN I HAD HER

TUNE: *Saw ye na my Peggy*

❧

From MMC.

❧

O gin I had her,
Ay gin I had her,
O gin I had her,
   Black altho' she be.
I wad lay her bale,
I'd gar her spew her kail;
She ne'er soud keep a mail,
   Till she dandl'd it on her knee.

She says, I am light
To manage matters right,
That I've nae might or weight
   To fill a lassie's ee;
But wad she tak a yokin',
I wad put a c—k in;
A quarter o't to flocken,
   I wad frankly gie.

i, 2.   MMC misprints "Ae"
i, 7.   mail, *i.e.* meal.
i, 8.   MMC misprints "Tell"

HE TILL'T AND SHE TILL'T

TUNE: *Maggie Lauder*

ᴏ◈ᴏ

From MMC.

ᴏ◈ᴏ

He till't, and she till't,
    An' a' to mak a lad again;
The auld beld carl,
    Whan he wan on did nod again;
An' he dang, an' she flang,
    An' a' to mak a laddie o't;
But he bor'd and she roar'd,
    An' coudna mak a lassie o't.

Line 4 MMC reads "When he wan on to nod again."

V

❧◆❧

ALIEN

MODES

Notes in this section are by
SYDNEY GOODSIR SMITH
unless otherwise initialled

TWEEDMOUTH TOWN

oᛨo

From MMC.

oᛨo

Near Tweedmouth town there liv'd three maids,
 Who used to tope good ale;
An' there likewise liv'd three wives,
 Who sometimes wagged their tale;
They often met, to tope an' chat,
 And tell odd tales of men;
[Cr]ying, when shall we meet again, an' again,
 [Cr]ying, when shall we meet again.

Not far from these there liv'd three widows,
 With complexions wan an' pale,
Who seldom used to tope an' bouse,
 An' seldom wagged their tale.
They sigh'd, they pin'd, they griev'd, they whin'd,
 An' often did complain,
Shall we, quo they, ne'er sport or play
 Nor wag our tails again, an' again.

Nine northern lads with their Scots plaids,
 By the Union, British call'd,
All nine-inch men, to a bousing came,
 Wi' their brawny backs I'm tald.
They all agreed, to cross the Tweed,
 An' ease them of their pain;
They laid them all down,
 An' they f—k'd them all round,
An' cross'd the Tweed again, an' again.

i, 7, 8.　Page cut. Maybe "Saying . . ."
iii, 4.　　MMC reads "backs an' tald."

[195]

THE BOWER OF BLISS

TUNE: *Logan Water*

From MMC. In a letter to William Stewart, Closeburn Castle, dated "Ellesland, Wednesday even:" [?9 July, 1788], Burns wrote: "I inclose you the Plenipo.—You will see another, The Bower of bliss; 'tis the work of a Revd Doctor of the Church of Scotland—Would [to] Heaven a few more of them would turn the[ir fie]ry Zeal *that way*! There, they might *spend* their Holy fury, and shew the *tree* by its *fruits*!!! There, the *in-bearing workings* might give hopeful presages of a *New-birth*!!!! The other two are by the author of the Plenipo, but 'The Doctor' is not half there, as I have mislaid it.—I have no copies left of either, so must have the precious pieces again" (DLF.*L* i, 232). M'Naught disingenuously remarks: "This shows the part played by the poet's boon companions in the compilation of the Crochallan collection"; but this is the only such contribution M'Naught points to—and an utterly uncharacteristic one, at that. It also shows, unfortunately, that the Bard really liked this sort of drivel. The present editors agree entirely with M'Naught when he says, "the 'high-kilted' muse does not become drawing-room costume. The deliberate, downright, mother-naked coarseness of the vernacular is infinitely preferable to this sickening stuff, which is Greek to the peasant, who calls a spade a spade because he has no other word for it."

Whilst others to thy bosom rise,
And paint the glories of thine eyes,
Or bid thy lips and cheeks disclose,
The unfading bloom of Eden's rose.
Less obvious charms my song inspire,
Which fell, not fear we most admire—
Less obvious charms, not less divine,
I sing that lovely bower of thine.

Rich gem! worth India's wealth alone,
How much pursued how little known;
Tho' rough its face, tho' dim its hue,
It soils the lustre of Peru.
The vet'ran such a prize to gain,
Might all the toils of war sustain;
The devotee forsake his shrine,
To venerate that bower of thine.

When the stung heart feels keen desire,
And through each vein pours liquid fire:
When with flush'd cheeks and burning eyes,
Thy lover to thy bosom flies;
Believe, dear maid, believe my vow,
By Venus' self, I swear, 'tis true!
More bright the higher beauties shine,
Illum'd by that strange bower of thine.

What thought sublime, what lofty strain
Its wond'rous virtues can explain?
No place how'er remote, can be
From its intense attraction free:
Tho' more elastic far than steel,
Its force ten thousand needles feel;
Pleas'd their high temper to resign,
In that magnetic bower of thine.

Irriguous vale, embrown'd with shades,
Which no intrinsic storm pervades!
Soft clime, where native summer glows,
And nectar's living current flows!
Not Tempe's vale, renowned of yore,
Of charms could boast such endless store;
More than Elysian sweets combine,
To grace that smiling bower of thine.

O, may no rash invader stain,
Love's warm, sequestered virgin fane!
For me alone let gentle fate,
Preserve the dear august retreat!
Along its banks when shall I stray?
Its beauteous landscape when survey?
How long in fruitless anguish pine,
Nor view unvail'd that bower of thine?

O! let my tender, trembling hand,
The awful gate of life expand!
With all its wonders feast my sight;
Dear prelude to immense delight!
Till plung'd in liquid joy profound,
The dark unfathom'd deep I sound;
All panting on thy breast recline,
And, murmuring, bless that bower of thine.

Last line. MMC has "bliss"

THE PLENIPOTENTIARY

TUNE: *The Terrible Law* or *Shawnbuee*

⌀❖⌀

From MM27. Not in MMC. Enclosed in same letter as "The Bower of Bliss"; it is certainly a cut above that horror. It was composed by Captain Morris, an ornament of the Carlton House set and author of *Songs Drinking, Political and Facetious* (c. 1790).

⌀❖⌀

The Dey of Algiers, when afraid of his ears,
A messenger sent to our court, sir,
As he knew in our state the women had weight,
He chose one well hung for the sport, sir.
He searched the Divan till he found out a man
Whose b—— were heavy and hairy,
And he lately came o'er from the Barbary shore
As the great Plenipotentiary.

When to England he came, with his p—— in a flame,
He showed it his Hostess on landing,
Who spread its renown thro' all parts of the town,
As a pintle past all understanding.
So much there was said of its snout and its head,
That they called it the great Janissary;
Not a lady could sleep till she got a sly peep
At the great Plenipotentiary.

As he rode in his coach, how the whores did approach,
And stared, as if stretched on a tenter;
He drew every eye of the dames that passed by,
Like the sun to its wonderful centre.
As he passed thro' the town not a window was down,
And the maids hurried out to the area,

The children cried, "Look, there's the man with the
    cock,
That's the great Plenipotentiary."

When he came to the Court, oh, what giggle and sport,
Such squinting and squeezing to view him,
What envy and spleen in the women were seen,
All happy and pleased to get to him.
They vowed from their hearts, if men of such parts
Were found on the coast of Barbary,
'Tis a shame not to bring a whole guard for the King,
Like the great Plenipotentiary.

The dames of intrigue formed their c—— in a league,
To take him in turns like good folk, sir;
The young misses' plan to was catch as catch can,
And all were resolved on a stroke, sir.
The cards to invite flew by thousands each night,
With bribes to the old secretary,
And the famous Eclipse was not let for more leaps
Than the great Plenipotentiary.

When his name was announced, how the women all
    bounced,
And their blood hurried up to their faces;
He made them all itch from navel to breech,
And their bubbies burst out all their laces;
There was such damned work to be f—— by the Turk,
That nothing their passion could vary;
All the nations [?matrons] fell sick for the Barbary
    p——
Of the great Plenipotentiary.

A Duchess whose Duke made her ready to puke,
With fumbling and f—— all night, sir,

Being first for the prize, was so pleased with its size,
That she begged for to stroke its big snout, sir.
My stars! cried her Grace, its head's like a mace,
'Tis as high as the Corsican Fairy;
I'll make up, please the pigs, for dry bobs and frigs,
With the great Plenipotentiary.

And now to be bor'd by this Ottoman Lord
Came a Virgin far gone in the wane, sir,
She resolved for to try, tho' her c—— was so dry,
That she knew it must split like a cane, sir.
True it was as she spoke, it gave way at each stroke,
But oh, what a woeful quandary!
With one terrible thrust her old piss-bladder burst
On the great Plenipotentiary.

The next to be tried was an Alderman's Bride,
With a c—— that would swallow a turtle,
She had horned the dull brows of her worshipful
    spouse,
Till they sprouted like Venus's myrtle.
Thro' thick and thro' thin, bowel deep he dashed in,
Till her c—— frothed like cream in a dairy,
And expressed by loud farts she was strained in all
    parts
By the great Plenipotentiary.

The next to be kissed, on the Plenipo's list,
Was a delicate Maiden of Honor,
She screamed at the sight of his p——, in a fright,
Tho' she'd had the whole palace upon her.
O Lord, she said, what a p—— for a maid!
Do, pray, come look at it, Cary!
But I *will* have one drive, if I'm ripped up alive,
By the great Plenipotentiary.

Two sisters next came, Peg and Molly by name,
Two ladies of very high breeding,
Resolved one should try, while the other stood by
And watch the amusing proceeding.
Peg swore by the gods that the Mussulman's cods
Were as big as both buttocks of Mary;
Molly cried with a grunt, he has ruined my c—
With his great Plenipotentiary.

The next for this plan was an old Haridan,
Who had swallowed huge p—— from each nation,
With over much use she had broken the sluice
'Twixt her —— and its lower relation.
But he stuck her so full that she roared like a bull,
Crying out she was bursting and weary,
So tight was she stuck by this wonderful f——
Of the great Plenipotentiary.

The next for a shag came the new Yankee flag;
Tho' lanky and scraggy in figure,
She was fond of the quid, for she had been well rid
From Washington down to a nigger.
Oh my! such a size! I guess it's first prize,
It's a wonder, quite next Ni-a-gary;
W-a-l-l, now I'm in luck, stranger, let's f——,
Bully for the great Plenipotentiary.

All heads were bewitched and longed to be stitched,
Even babies would languish and linger,
And the boarding-school Miss, as she sat down to piss,
Drew a Turk on the floor with her finger.
For fancied delight, they all clubbed for a shite,
To frig in the school necessary,
And the Teachers from France f—— à la distance
With the great Plenipotentiary.

Each sluice-c——d bawd, who'd been s——d abroad
Till her premises gaped like a grave, sir,
Found luck was so thick, she could feel the Turk's
    p——,
Tho' all others were lost in her cave, sir.
The nymphs of the stage did his ramrod engage,
Made him free of their gay seminary;
And the Italian Signors opened all their back doors
To the great Plenipotentiary.

Then of love's sweet reward, measured out by the yard,
The Turk was most blest of mankind, sir,
For his powerful dart went right home to the heart,
Whether stuck in before or behind, sir.
But no pencil can draw this great-pintled Bashaw,
Then let each c—— loving contemporary,
As cocks of the game, let's drink to the name
Of the great Plenipotentiary.

UNA'S LOCK

o◇o

From MM27. Not in MMC. Included in *The Giblet Pye* (c. 1806).
Burns wrote to George Thomson in September, 1794 (DLF, *L*
II, 256), enclosing the song "Sae flaxen were her ringlets"
(HH III, 160):

Do you know . . . a blackguard Irish song called "Oonagh's
Waterfall, or The lock that scattered Oonagh's p-ss"? . . .
—I have often regretted the want of decent verses to it . . .
you may be pleased to have some verses to it that you may
sing it to the Ladies.

o◇o

'Twas on a sweet morning,
    When violets were a-springing,
The dew the meads adorning,
    The larks melodious singing;
The rose-trees, by each breeze,
    Were gently wafted up and down,
And the primrose, that then blows,
    Bespangled nature's verdant gown.
The purling rill, the murmuring stream,
    Stole gently through the lofty grove:
Such was the time when Darby stole
    Out to meet his barefoot love.

Tol, lol, &c.

Sweet Una was the tightest,
    Genteelest of the village dames;
Her eyes were the brightest
    That e'er set youthful heart in flames.
Her lover to move her
    By every art in man essay'd
In ditty, for pity,
    This lovely maid he often prayed,

But she, perverse, his suit deni'd.
  Sly Darby, being enraged at this,
Resolv'd when next they met to seize
  The lock that scatters Una's piss.

        Tol, lol, &c.

Beneath a lofty spreading oak
  She sat with can and milking pail;
From lily hands at each stroke
  In flowing streams the milk did steal.
With peeping, and creeping,
  Sly Darby now comes on apace;
In raptures the youth sees
  The blooming beauties of her face.
Fir'd with her charms, he now resolv'd
  No longer to delay his bliss,
But instantly to catch the lock
  That scatters pretty Una's piss.

        Tol, lol, &c.

Upon her back he laid her,
  Turned up her smock so lily white;
With joy the youth surveyed her,
  Then gaped with wonder and delight.
Her thighs they were so snowy fair,
  And just between appeared a crack;
The lips red, and overspread
  With curling hair of jetty black.
Transported now, Darby beholds
  The sum of all his promised bliss,
And instantly he caught the lock
  That scatters pretty Una's piss.

        Tol, lol, &c.

Within his arms he seized her,
    And pressed her to his panting breast;
What more could have appeased her,
    But oaths which Darby meant in jest.
He swore he'd but adore her,
    And to her ever constant prove;
He'd wed her, he'd bed her,
    And none on earth but her he'd love.
With vows like those he won her o'er,
    And hoped she'd take it not amiss
If he presumed to catch the lock
    That scatters pretty Una's piss.
                Tol, lol, &c.

His cock it stood erected,
    His breeches down about his heels,
And what he long expected
    He now with boundless rapture feels.
Now entered, and concentred,
    The beauteous maid lay in a trance,
His bullocks went like elbows
    Of fiddlers in a country dance.
The melting Una, now she cries,
    I'd part with life for joy like this;
With showers of bliss they jointly oiled
    The lock that scatters Una's piss.
                Tol, lol, &c.

VI

✣

LIBEL
SUMMONS

LIBEL SUMMONS

The British Museum has three MSS of this poem, known also as "The Court of Equity" and "The Fornicator's Court." MS A—Egerton MS 1656, folios 8a–10a—has the fullest text, totalling 160 lines. MS B—Egerton MS 1656, folio 11a–b—is a fragment, containing only the first 57 lines of the poem. MS C—Additional MS 22307: the Hastie Collection of Burns MSS, folios 176a–177b—is a shorter version of only 110 lines.

The present text is Hans Hecht's collation of the three MSS, as printed in *Archiv für das Studium der Neueren Sprachen und Literaturen*, Vol. CXXX (1913), pp. 67ff. It follows MS A, with one couplet from MS B inserted in brackets. The most important variants in MS C are given in footnotes. [DFL]

Written by Burns for the Tarbolton Bachelors' Club in 1786. A version is included as MS addendum by Scott Douglas in MMC. [SGS]

In Truth and Honor's name, AMEN.—
Know all men by these presents plain.—

This twalt o' May at M[auchli]ne given;
The year 'tween eighty five an' seven;
We, FORNICATORS by profession,
As per extractum from each Session;[1]

And by our BRETHREN constituted,
A COURT of Equity deputed:
With special authoris'd direction,
To take beneath our strict protection,
The stays-unlacing, quondam maiden,

---

[1] In MS C this couplet follows here:

In way and manner here narrated
Pro bono Amor congregated

With growing life and anguish laden;
Who by the Scoundrel is deny'd
Who led her thoughtless steps aside.—[1]

The knave who takes a private stroke
Beneath his sanctimonious cloke:
(The Coof wha stan's on clishmaclavers
When lasses hafflins offer favors)[2]

All who in any way or manner
Distain the FORNICATOR's honor,
We take cognisance there anent
The proper Judges competent.—
First, Poet B[urns], he takes the CHAIR,
Allow'd by all, his title's fair;
And past nem. con. without dissension,
He has a DUPLICATE pretension.—

The second, Sm[i]th, our worthy FISCAL,
To cowe each pertinacious rascal;
In this, as every other state,
His merit is conspicuous great;
R[ichmo]nd the third, our trusty CLERK,
Our minutes regular to mark,
And sit dispenser of the law,

In MS C the next eight lines read as follows:
>He who disowns the ruin'd Fair-one,
>And for her wants and woes does care none;
>The wretch that can refuse subsistence
>To those whom he has given existence;
>He who when at a lass's by-job,
>Defrauds her wi' a fr-g or dry-b-b;
>The coof that stands on clishmaclavers.
>When women haflins offer favors:—

[2] From MS B.

In absence of the former twa.—
The fourth, our MESSENGER AT ARMS,
When failing all the milder terms,
Hunt[e]r, a hearty willing Brother,
Weel skill'd in dead an' living leather.—

Without preamble less or more said,
We, BODY POLITIC aforesaid,
With legal, due WHEREAS and WHEREFORE,
We are appointed here to care for
The int'rests of our Constituents,
And punish contravening Truants;
To keep a proper regulation
Within the lists of FORNICATION.—

WHEREAS, Our FISCAL, by petition,
Informs us there is strong suspicion
YOU, Coachman DOW, and Clockie BROWN,
Baith residenters in this town,
In other words, you, Jock and Sandie
Hae been at wark at HOUGHMAGANDIE;
And now when it is come to light,
The matter ye deny outright.—

You CLOCKIE BROWN, there's witness borne,
And affidavit made and sworne,
That ye hae rais'd a hurlie-burlie
In Maggy Mitchel's tirlie-whurlie.—
(And blooster'd at her regulator,
Till a' her wheels gang clitter-clatter.—)[1]

An' farther still, ye cruel Vandal,
A tale might e'en in Hell be scandal,
Ye've made repeated wicked tryals

[1] From MS C.

With drugs an' draps in doctor's phials,
Mix'd, as ye thought, wi' fell infusion,
Your ain begotten wean to poosion.
An' yet ye are sae scant o' grace,
Ye daur set up your brazen face,
An' offer for to tak your aith,
Ye never lifted Maggie's claith.—
But tho' by Heaven an' Hell ye swear,
Laird Wilson's sclates can witness bear,
Ae e'ening of a M[auchli]ne fair,
That Maggie's masts, they saw them bare,
For ye had furl'd up her sails,
An' was at play at heads an' tails.—

You COACHMAN DOW are here indicted
To have, as publickly ye're wyted,
Been clandestinely upward-whirlan
The petticoats o' Maggie Borlan;
An' gied her canister a rattle,
That months to come it winna settle.—
An' yet ye offer your protest,
Ye never harry'd Maggie's nest;
Tho' it's weel-kend that, at her gyvle,
Ye hae gien mony a kytch an' kyvle.—

Then BROWN & DOW, above-design'd,
For clags and clauses there subjoin'd,
We COURT *aforesaid, cite & summon,*
That on the fourth o' June in comin,
The hour o' Cause, in our Courtha'
At Whiteford's arms, ye answer LAW!

But, as reluctantly we punish,
An' rather, mildly would admonish:
Since Better Punishment prevented,
Tham OBSTINACY sair repented.—

Then, for that *ancient Secret's sake*,
Ye have the honor to partake;
An' for that *noble Badge* you wear,
You, SANDIE DOW, our BROTHER dear,
We give you as a MAN an' MASON,
This private, sober, friendly lesson.—

Your crime, a manly deed we view it.
As *man alone* can only do it;
But, in denial, persevering,
Is to a *Scoundrel's name* adhering.
The best of *men* hae been surpris'd;
The best o' *women* been advis'd:
Nay, *cleverest Lads* hae haen a trick o't,
An' *bonniest Lasses* taen a lick o't.—
Then Brother Dow, if you're asham'd
In such a QUORUM to be nam'd,
Your conduct much is to be blam'd.—
See, ev'n *himsel*—there's godly BRYAN,
The auld *whatreck* he has been tryin;
When such as he put to their han',
What man or character need stan'?
Then Brother dear, lift up your brow,
And, like yoursel, the truth avow;
Erect a dauntless face upon it,
An' say, "I am the man has done it;
"I Sandie Dow gat Meg wi' wean,
"An's fit to do as much again."

Ne'er mind their solemn rev'rend faces,
Had they—in proper times an' places,
But *seen & fun'*—I muckle dread it,
They just would done as you & we did.—
To tell the truth's a manly lesson,
An' doubly proper in a MASON.—

You MONSIEUR BROWN, as it is proven,
Meg Mitchel's wame by you was hoven;
Without you by a quick repentence
Acknowledge Meg's an' your acquaintance,
Depend on't, this shall be your sentence.—
Our Beadles to the Cross shall take you,
And there shall mither naked make you;
Some canie grip near by your middle,
They shall it bind as tight's a fiddle;
The raep they round the pump shall tak
An' tye your hans behint your back;
Wi' just an ell o' string allow'd
To jink an' hide you frae the croud.
There shall ye stan', a legal seizure.
Induring Maggie Mitchel's pleasure;
So be, her pleasure dinna pass
Seven turnings of a half-hour glass:
Nor shall it in her pleasure be
To louse you out in less than three.—
This, our futurum esse DECREET,
We mean it not to keep a secret;
But in OUR SUMMONS here insert it,
And whoso dares, may controvert it.—
This, mark'd before the date and place is;
Subsignum est per B[urns] the Praeses.—
                                    L.S.B.

This summons & the Signet mark
Extractum est per R[ichmon]d, Clerk.—
                        R . . . . d.
At M[auchli]ne, twenty fifth o' May,
About the twalt hour o' the day,[1]

---

[1] In MS C these lines read:

> At MAUCHLINE, idem date of June,
> Tween six & seven, the afternoon,

and the date in line 3 (p. 209) is "This fourth o' June."

You two in propria personae
Before design'd Sandie & Johnie,
This SUMMONS legally have got,
As vide witness underwrote;
Within the house of John D[ow], Vintner,
Nunc facio hoc—
                    Gullelmus Hun[te]r.

GLOSSARY

ᴼᐧᗘᐧᴼ

A', *all*
Abee, *me be*
Aboon, *above*
Ae, *one*
Aff, *off*
Aften, *often*
Again, *against*
Aiblens, *perhaps*
Aik, *an oak*
Ain, *own*
Airt, *direction; to direct*
Aith, *an oath*
Aits, *oats*
Alane, *alone*
An, *if*
Ance, *once*
Ane, *one*
An's, *and is; and his*
Arle, *pledge*
Arselins, *backwards*
As due as, *whenever*
Atweesh, *between*
Awa, *away*
Awe, *to owe*
Awee, *a little time*
Ayont, *beyond*

Bad, *bid*
Bade, *endured; desired; persuaded*
Bairn'd, *got with child*
Baith, *both*
Bann'd, *cursed*
Bane, *bone*
Bang, *a stroke*
Bauld, *bold*
Bawsent, *white-streaked on face*
Be, *by*
Bear, *barley*
Bed-stock, *bedside; wooden bar at front of box bed*
Befa', *befall*
Behint, *behind*
Belang, *belong to*

Beld, *bald*
Belyve, *by and by*
Ben, *inside; the inner room*
Bends, *bounds*
Bent, *coarse grass near sea*
Be't, *be it*
Bicker, *beaker; move quickly*
Bide, *to stand, to endure*
Bien (of a person), *well-to-do;* (of a place), *comfortable*
Bigget, biggit, *built*
Birkie, *fellow*
Birss, *hair; bristle*
Blatter, *attack*
Blaw, *to blow; to brag*
Bleerie, *bleary-eyed; small beer*
Blin', *blind*
Blooster, *bluster*
Blyth, *happily*
Bock, *to spew; to vomit*
Boddle, *one-sixth of a penny*
Boost, *must needs*
Bort, *bored*
Bousing, *drinking*
Bowe, *bowl*
Brae, *slope of a hill*
Braid, *cloth*
Brak, *did break*
Braulies, *splendidly*
Braw, *fine; handsome*
Brawly's, *finely as*
Broads, *shutters*
Brose, *porridge*
Browst, *a brewing*
Brunt, *burnt*
Brust, *burst*
Buckl'd, *curled*
Busk, *bush; dress*
Buskit, *dressed; decked*
But(t), *without; wanting; only; outer room*
Buttock-hire, *penance*
Byke, *hive*

[217]

Byre-en', *cowshed end*

Ca', *to drive; call; summon*
Ca' throu', *to push forward*
Cadger, *a carrier*
Caller, *fresh*
Cam, *came*
Cameronian, *Presbyterian sect*
Canie, *careful*
Canty, *cheerful*
Carl, *a man*
Carlin, *an old woman*
Cauld, *cold*
Chap, *to knock*
Chaup, *a blow*
Chiel, *young fellow*
Chitterling, *shirt frill*
Chuckies, *chickens*
Claes, *clothes; covers*
Clag, *burden*
Claise, *clothes*
Claith, *cloth*
Clamb, *climbed*
Clappin', *fondling*
Clash, *gossip; to talk*
Clatter, *to talk idly; gossip*
Claught, *clutched*
Claut, *rake*
Claw, *to scratch; to fondle*
Cleek, *hook*
Clegs, *spurs*
Clew, *scratched; fondled*
Clishmaclavers, *idle talk*
Clocken-hen, *broody hen*
Cloot, *hoof*
Clout, *mend; patch*
Clouts, *clothes*
Clue, *cleuch, narrow glen*
Coal-riddle, *sieve*
Coft, *bought*
Coggin', *wedging*
Cogie, *a small wooden pail*
Coof, *a fool*
Coost, *did cast off*
Coost out, *quarrelled*
Coup, *to overturn; a fall*
Courtha', *court hall*
Cow, *coward*
Cowe, *to crop; to subdue; horror*
Cow'd, *cropped*
Crack, *gossip*
Crap, *crept; a crop*

Craw, *to crow*
Creel, *a basket*
Crowdie, *curds; cheese*
Cuttie, *little*
Cuttie-gun, *short tobacco pipe*
Cuttie-mun, *old song*
Cuttie stoup, *short drinks*

Dae, *do*
Daffin, *sporting*
Dang, *pushed; knocked*
Darge, *day's work*
Daud, *a lump; a large piece*
Daunton, *awe*
Daur, *dare*
Dawtin', *petting*
Deevil's dizzen, *13 inches*
Deil, *the devil*
Dibble, *tool*
Ding, *to shove; to hit*
Dinna, *do not*
Ditty, *indictment*
Dizzen, *dozen*
Docht, *could*
Dock, *tail*
Dockins, *dock leaves*
Dod, *jog*
Doit, *mite*
Dool, *a blow; sorrowful*
Doudled, *dandled*
Dought na, *dared not*
Dow, *do; can*
Dow, *a pigeon*
Downa-do, *old age*
Down-cod, *feather pillow*
Draik, *to soak*
Dree, *to bear; to endure*
Dreep, *to drip*
Druken, *drunken*
Dud, Duddie, *ragged*
Duntie, *thump*
Dunts, *strokes; blows; knocks*
Durk, *a dagger*
Dyke-back, *back of the wall*

Eastlin, *eastern*
Ee, *eye; to watch*
Een or ein, *eyes*
Eith, *easy*
Elekit, *of the Elect*
En', *end*

[218]

Fa', *enjoy; fall*
Fae, *foe*
Fa'en, *fallen*
Fairin', *food*
Fand, *found*
Fash, *heed*
Fash'd, *vexed*
Fauld, *folded; a fold*
Fauteors a', *offenders all*
Fau't, *fault*
Fau'tor, *offender*
Fauts, *faults*
Fee, *wage; to hire*
Feetie, *feet*
Fidge, *to exert*
Fient a, *devil a*
Fin', *find*
Fistles, *fizzes; fidgets*
Fit, *foot*
Fit-man, *footman*
Fitstead, *footstep*
Flaes, *fleas; flies*
Flang, *struggled; heaved; flung*
Flate, *protested*
Fley'd, *afraid*
Flowe, *morass*
Fly'd, *frightened*
Flytin, *scolding*
Fodgel'd, *heaved; shook*
Foggie, *mossy*
Foot, *speed*
Forbye, *besides*
Forgat, *forgot*
Fou, *full; drunk*
Frae, *from*
Fu', *full; drunk*
Fun', *found*
Fur *or* furr, *furrow*
Fyke, *fidget; bustle*

Gae, *go; gave*
Gaed *or* gade, *went*
Gager, *gauger, exciseman*
Gain', *against*
Gair, *gusset*
Gamon, *petticoat; legs*
Gang, *to go*
Gar, *to make; to compel; to cause to*
Gard, *past tense of* Gar
Garse, *grass*
Gart it clink, *made it chime*
Gart me, *got me to*

Gat, *got*
Gate, *road*
Gaud, *goad*
Gaun, *going*
Gavel, *gable*
Gear, *wealth, goods; harness*
Gerse, *grass*
Gets, *children; brats*
Gie, *give*
Gied me the glaiks, *jilted me*
Gif, *if*
Gin, *if*
Girdin', *driving; exercise*
Girt, *girded; girth; large*
Gizzen, *dry up*
Glaur, *muck, mud*
Gled, *buzzard; kite*
Glowran, *gazing*
Goosset, *gusset*
Goud *or* gowd, *gold*
Gowan, *daisies*
Graipit, *groped; examined; searched*
Graith, *equipment; gear*
Grane, *groan*
Grat, *wept*
Gravat, *muffler*
Greetie, *crying*
Gripet, *grasped*
Groazle, *grunt*
Gully, *cut; stab; poke*
Gyvel *or* gyvle, *hind parts; gable*

Ha', *hall*
Had, *hold*
Hae, *have*
Hadin', *leading*
Haen, *had*
Hafflins, *partially; halfway*
Hair, *corn*
Haith, *faith!*
Haly, *holy*
Haly band, *kirk session*
Hame, *home*
Han', *hand*
Hanger, *dagger*
Hard, *heard*
Haud, *hold*
Hawkie, *white faced cow*
Heigh, *high*
Her lane, *alone; by herself*
Herryin', *robbing*
Hie, *high*

Hing, *hang*
Hinnie, *honey*
Hissie or hizzie, *girl; hussie*
Holland-sark, *linen shift*
Hotch, *shove; jerk*
Hough, *thigh*
Houghmagandie, *fornication*
Hoven, *swollen*
Howe, *hollow*
Howk, *dig*
Hoy'd, *hailed*
Hurchin, *hedgehog*
Hurdies, *buttocks*
Hurdies fyke, *buttocks in action*
Hurly, *storm*

Ilk, ilka, *each, every*
Ither, *each one; other*
Ither, *adder*
Its lane, *by itself*
I's no, *I'll not*
Itsel, *itself*

Jad, *a jade*
Jander, *to chatter*
Jimp, *slender, neat*
Jink, *to dodge*
Jirts, *jerks*
Jo, *sweetheart; joy*

Kail, *soup; broth*
Kecklin, *cackling*
Keep out, *watch out*
Ken, *know*
Kend, *knew; known*
Kill, *kiln*
Kimmer, *woman, girl, wench*
Kimmerland, *womankind*
Kintra, *country*
Kipples, *coupling*
Kirst'nin', *christening*
Kittle, *ticklish, difficult; dangerous; tricky*
Knocking-stone, *stone mortar for hulling barley*
Knowe, *knoll; hillock*
Koontrie, *country*
Kye, *cattle*
Kytch, *toss*
Kyvle, *tumble*

Labour lee, *plough grassland*

Labster, *lobster*
Laft, *loft*
Laigh, *low*
Laik, *lack*
Lair, *bog*
Laithron doup, *lazy rump*
Lane, *alone (see* Her 1., Its 1.)
Lang's, *long as*
Langsyne saunts, *saints of long ago*
Lap, *leapt*
Lat, *let*
Lave, *the rest*
Laverock, *the lark*
Lea's, *leaves*
Lee-rig, *untilled field*
Leuch or leugh, *laughed*
Licket, *have licked*
Lien, *lain*
Liltit, *pulled*
Linkin', *sprightly*
Links, *locks*
Loan, *lane*
Lo'e, loo, *love*
Loon, loun, *fellow; lad*
Loot, *let (past)*
Loups, *leaps*
Lous'd, *loosened*
Louse, *to loosen*
Lowe, *blaze*
Lown, *lad*
Lowse, *to loosen, let loose*
Lucky, *goodwife; alewife*
Lug, *to pull*
Lugs, *ears*

Mae, *more*
Mail, *meal; male*
Mair, *more*
Maist, *almost; most*
Mak, *make*
Make, *like, equal, peer*
Mallison, *curse*
Mane, *moan*
Mantie, *cloth*
Margh, *marrow*
Ma't, *malt*
Maukin, *a hare*
Maun, *must*
Maunna, *must not*
Meal-pocks, *meal bags*
Meikle, *much*
Mess, *minister*

Midden wa', *dunghill wall*
Mim-mou'd, *mealymouthed*
Minnie, *mother*
Misca'd, *abused*
Modeworck *or* modiewark, *mole*
Mou', *mouth*
Moulie, *soft; earthy*
Mowe, *copulate*
Muckle, *big; much*
Muir, *moor*

Naething, *nothing*
Naigs, *nags*
Na mony, *few*
Nane, *none*
Neebor, *neighbour*
Neep, *turnip*
Neist *or* niest, *next*
Neive *or* nieve, *fist*
Nerse, *tail*
Nicher, *whinny; snigger*
Nidge't, *squeezed*
Nine, *nine inches long*
Nits, *nuts*
Nocht, *nothing*
Nyvel, *navel*

Onie *or* ony, *any*
Or, *before*
O't, *of it*
Ousen, *oxen*
Owsen-staw, *ox stall*

Pat, *put*
Pat it in my will, *gave me my way*
Pegh, *puff*
Pickle, *little; grain of corn*
Pickle hair, *last corn cut*
Pillie, *male organ*
Pintle, *pipe; male organ*
Pit, *put*
Pith, *strength*
Plack, *a third of a penny*
Playing bye, *being false to*
Pock, *bag*
Pockie, *small sac*
Poosion, *poison*
Pounie, pownie, *pony*
Pow, *the head; to pull*
Prie, *to accept; to taste*
Pry, *to try; to taste*
Pu'd, *pulled*

Quarter, *one-quarter yard; 9 inches*
Quech, *two-eared cup*
Quine, *lass; wench*
Quo', *quoth*

Raep, *rope*
Rair, *roar*
Rase, *rose*
Rash, *a rush*
Raxin, *reaching*
Ream, *foam*
Rede, *advise*
Reek, *smoke*
Rig, *field, ridge, furrow*
Ring, *reign*
Ripples, *backache*
Rive, *tear*
Roaring-pin, *rolling pin*
Rock, *a distaff*
Rough, *plentiful*
Roughness, *brushwood*
Row, *roll up; wrap*
Rowted, *bellowed*
Rowth, *plenty*
Rug, *tug*
Runt, *cabbage stalk*

Sae, *so*
Saft, *soft*
Sair, *to serve; sore; sorely; severe; very much*
Saird, *served*
Sairest, *hardest*
Sangs, *songs*
Sark, *shift; shirt; chemise*
Sa'tty, *salty*
Saunt, *saint*
Scauld, *scold*
Scauls, *scolds*
Sclates, *slates*
Sel, *self*
Sell'd, *sold*
Shaw, *show*
Sheds, *divides, parts, separates*
Sherra, *sheriff*
Shillin hill, *winnowing hill*
Shoen, shoon, *shoes*
Sic, *such*
Siccan a, *such a*
Sicker, *sure*
Side and wide, *large and low-hung*

[221]

Siller, *money; silver*
Sin, *since*
Sinnens, *sinews*
Sinsyne, *since then*
Skelpit doup, *slapped rump*
Sma', *small; thin*
Sock, *ploughshare*
Sodger, soger *or* sojer, *soldier*
Sonsy, *lively, blooming, hale*
Soud, *should*
Souple, *yielding; to make supple; to soak*
Sowen-pat, *gruel pot*
Spak, *spoke*
Speel, *climb*
Spier, *ask*
Spretty bush, *clump of rushes*
Stane, *stone*
Stane o' stanin' graith, *set of good equipment*
Stang, *sting*
Stanin', *standing; hesitantly*
Stan't themlane, *stood by themselves*
Stark, *strong*
Starns, *stars*
Staund, *set*
Staunin', *standing; erect*
Steer, *stir; arouse*
Stell'd, *braced*
Sten, *leap*
Stented graith, *harnessed the plough*
Steward, *housekeeper*
Stibble, *stubble*
Stilts, *shafts*
Stown't, *stolen it*
Strack, *struck*
Straik, *stroke*
Straik o't, *shot at it*
Strang, *strong*
Strunt, *spirits*
Succar, succour, *sugar; sugary*
Swats, *small beer*
Sykie risk, *watery marsh*
Syne, *then; since*

Tae, *too; to; toe*
Taen, *taken*
Tald, *told*
Taper, *shapely*
Tappit hen, *jug containing a Scots quart* (=3 *English quarts*)

Tell'd, *told*
Tent, *attend*
Term-day, *Whitsunday; Martinmas*
Tham, *them*
Theekit, *thatched*
Thegither, *together*
Thie, *thigh*
Thirl, *thrill*
Thole, *endure*
Thrang, *full; thronged*
Thrave, 24 *sheaves of grain*
Thretty, *thirty*
Thumpin, *buxom*
Tight, *shapely, trim, sound*
Tither, *t'other*
Till, *to*
Till't, *tilled; "went to it"*
Tinkler, *tinker*
Tine, tint, *lose, lost*
Tirliewirlies, *ornaments*
Tittling, *sparrow*
Titty, *sister*
Tocher, *dowry*
Todlen, *toddling*
Toop-horn, *ram's horn*
Touzle, *dishevel*
Trams, *shafts*
Trogger, *a pedlar*
Trow, *to swear; believe*
Trow'd, *rolled over*
True, *to believe, to trust*
Twa, *two*
Twalt, *twelfth*
Tway thumb-bread, *two thumbs' breadth*
Twynin', *weaving; parting*

Unco, *uncommon; great; strange*
Unkenned, *unknown*

Vera, *very*
Verra crack, *instant*

Wa', *a wall*
Wad, *would; would have; wed*
Wae gae by, *woe to*
Waes me, *alas, woe is me*
Waft, *to weave; weft or woof*
Waigles, *waggles*
Wakin', *walking*
Waled, *picked*

Waly, *well*
Wame, *belly*
Wan, *won*
Want, *lack; lose*
Wants the, *has no*
Wap, *wrap*
Wark, *work*
Warld, *world*
Warst, *worst*
Wast, *west*
Wat, *to know; wet*
Wauken'd, *wakened*
Waukin, *awake*
Waulies, *the buttocks*
Waur, *worse*
Waur't, *worried*
Waxen wan, *grown feeble*
Wean, *child*
Wearin', *using*
Weary fa', *curses on*
Webster, *weaver*
Wee, *little; a bit; a short period of time*
Wee coat, *petticoat*
Weel, *well*
Weel-knoozed, *well-kneaded*
Weet, *splash-board; wet*

Weetin', *wetting*
Weir, *war; might*
Whang, *tape; lace; a large slice*
Whatreck, *weasel*
What she could bicker, *as fast as she could*
Whiltie-whaltie, *in a state of palpitation*
Whittle, *knife*
Whyles, *sometimes*
Wight, *brisk*
Wi little wark, *easily*
Wimble bores, *small holes*
Win', *wind*
Windy-wa's, *windy walls; a boaster*
Winna, *will not*
Wordy, *worthy*
Wyte, *blame*

Yeard, *yard*
Yerk, *to drive; to jerk*
Ye'se, *you shall; you will*
Yill, *ale*
Yin, *one*
Yokin', *a stint; a bout*
Yorlin, *a finch; yellow hammer*